"Deeply grounded in the worl
together the most ancient wisd
of life, allowing us to read ove.
book for the generations. As beautifully written as it is profoundly true, *The Wise Leader* is for everyone who leads, for everyone who someday will lead."

—**Steven Garber**
senior fellow for vocation and the common good at
M.J. Murdock Charitable Trust and author of
The Seamless Life: A Tapestry of Love and Learning, Worship and Work

"I know of no other book quite like this one. For the past six years, I've watched Uli Chi's thinking evolve as we've cotaught a seminary course on 'wise leadership.' Uli sees wisdom through multiple prisms, including art, marketplace, Scripture, literature, and personal narrative. The result is remarkable."

—**Alec Hill**
president emeritus of InterVarsity Christian Fellowship/USA

"In a time when we are bombarded by dizzying amounts of information, the wisdom most needed to navigate a complex, fast-changing and often confusing world is increasingly rare. Out of the deep and refreshing well of a well-lived life, Uli Chi offers timeless and priceless wisdom essential for the flourishing of any leadership enterprise. I am deeply grateful that this wisdom is now available in this wonderful book. I highly recommend it."

—**Tom Nelson**
president of Made to Flourish and author of
Work Matters, The Economics of Neighborly Love, and *The Flourishing Pastor*

"Uli draws powerfully on his own professional experiences sharing his failures as poignantly as approaches that worked well. This is a must read for any aspiring leader who wants to bring a Christian understanding into the challenging and ambiguous world of effective leadership."

—**Peter Shaw**
chair of Praesta Partners, UK

"This is a book that does not so much define 'wisdom' as allow it to unfold. As we read through the book we observe different fabrics—visual art, biblical teaching, fantasy literature, poetry, business books and articles, and more—knit together with examples from Uli's own career until a truly multifaceted image of the wise leader emerges."

—**Jeff Van Duzer**
author of *Why Business Matters to God (And What Still Needs to Be Fixed)*

"Filled with practical guidance, this is a book that will seep into your soul and change you."

—**Denise Daniels**
Hudson T. Harrison Endowed Chair of Entrepreneurship
at Wheaton College

"Reflecting on biblical truth and his experience of leading in diverse contexts, Uli guides us on the journey to wisdom. Some of what he writes will be reassuringly familiar. Some will be surprising, even unsettling, as you experience the chasm that exists between cultural norms and godly wisdom. *The Wise Leader* will invite you to embrace and embody the 'wisdom from above' that will enable you to be a wise leader."

—**Mark D. Roberts**
senior strategist of the Max De Pree Center for Leadership

"Books on leadership are a dime a dozen, typically with a laundry list of to-dos. *The Wise Leader* is different! Uli Chi has written a profoundly personal and inspired account of wisdom being essential to leadership. This book will help readers navigate the joys, frustrations, pressures, and ambiguities of leadership in new, hopeful, and life-giving ways."

—**Ross Stewart**
dean of the School of Business, Government,
and Economics at Seattle Pacific University

"Wisdom is easier to experience than to define. Working with Uli is an experience in wisdom and humility. Uli has shown us how wisdom is not just a virtue, but a practice expressed in relationship with God, family, friends, colleagues, and neighbors."

—**Clive Lim**
founder and managing director of Leap International

"Drawing on a lifetime of wide-ranging leadership, *The Wise Leader* articulates an integrative vision of leadership that is spiritually alert, biblically serious, and practically grounded. This book should be required reading for Christians who strive to serve God in their varied leadership responsibilities in every sector of society."

—**Jeffrey P. Greenman**
president of Regent College, Vancouver

THE
WISE
LEADER

ULI CHI

WILLIAM B. EERDMANS PUBLISHING COMPANY
GRAND RAPIDS, MICHIGAN

Wm. B. Eerdmans Publishing Co.
4035 Park East Court SE, Grand Rapids, Michigan 49546
www.eerdmans.com

Book design by Lydia Hall

Printed in the United States of America

30 29 28 27 26 25 24   1 2 3 4 5 6 7

ISBN 978-0-8028-8404-6

Library of Congress Cataloging-in-Publication Data

A catalog record for this book is available from the Library of Congress.

Portions of this work previously appeared in *Life for Leaders*, a publication of
the De Pree Center at Fuller Theological Seminary.

Excerpts from "East Coker" and "Little Gidding," from *Four Quartets* by T. S.
Eliot. Copyright 1936 by Houghton Mifflin Harcourt Publishing Company,
renewed 1964 by T. S. Eliot. Copyright 1940, 1941, 1942 by T. S. Eliot, renewed
1968, 1969, 1970 by Esme Valerie Eliot. Used by permission of HarperCollins
Publishers and Faber and Faber Ltd.

In some instances names and identifying details have been omitted or altered
to protect anonymity.

Contents

FOREWORD

Wisdom is truth and character lived in context. When each of those dimensions is at play, we have the makings of wisdom, whether conscious or otherwise. In other words, we are living into and out of the depths of life and love itself—for our benefit and for that of the people and world around us.

This profound and moving book by Uli Chi takes us on an inner and expansive exploration of wisdom, specially considered for the life of the leader. This is not a book of aphorisms with "Ten Tips" on wisdom. This is the real thing because Chi is wise. To start with, he lives, leads, and writes with the humility that is fundamental to a life of wisdom. With the belief that "the fear of the Lord is the beginning of wisdom," Chi's life is grounded in the wisdom of God's own being and revelation in Scripture, and incarnate in "the Word/[Wisdom] made flesh": Jesus Christ. At the same time, this does not make the wisdom he explores "religious" or exclusively for the benefit of Christians. He is entirely aware that many readers share a common hunger for wisdom, even as we all live in a pluralist world. Chi's assumption is that wisdom arises from reality itself, which explains why it is capacious and trustworthy enough for anyone.

The pursuit of wisdom has shaped Chi's life as a business and technology leader and as a person, innovator, employee, founder, problem solver, employer, and CEO. Perceptive insight, careful listening, and steady and responsive discernment have all been aspects of how he has tried, in humility and without perfection, to live and lead with wisdom. His many examples and experiences of this arduous process are varied and practical. Wisdom is not for life in midair but for life and work on the ground. As a learner, out of strengths and vulnerabilities, times of thriving and of struggle, Chi allows us to see up close and in person the freedom and growth that the pursuit of wisdom invites and requires. The insights he shares call us away from being caught in the corners of our own making, away from unnecessary binaries, and into true collaboration, a diminishment of fear, and the creativity and imagination that leadership needs. For Chi, wisdom is capacious and hopeful even as it is honest and realistic.

It's no wonder, then, that Chi has been sought after to serve on and lead various boards. Businesses, organizations, and institutions are voracious for wise leaders to help guide and lead. There is no end to the need, but there can be a shortage of supply. Just as the true wisdom Chi encourages can inform every level of employee, so it can and should inform a board or any group of friends or collaborators. The wisdom to which Chi points has to do with listening, mutuality, humility, discernment, and community. This requires open, honest, trusting conversation that draws from the deep wells of character and discernment. Such work arises from character, self-awareness, and self-criticism. It comes from a diversity of perspectives of depth and range, gathered around the welfare of a common enterprise. Chi depicts and describes this dynamic in its vulnerability, challenges, and importance—all of which underscore the need for wisdom.

As husband, father, brother in the faith, leader and teacher in the church, and in other faith-related organizations, Chi also bears witness to the needs and relevance of embodied wisdom. In these contexts too the internal dimensions of wise character in action are needed. The purpose of corporate worship is the discovery and renewal of the God whose life "holds all things together" and informs the who, the why, and the how of living and of faith. What may be implicit throughout the rhythms and responsibilities of everyday life becomes overt and explicit in the context of Christian communion with God and one another—for its own sake and for the sake of the world in which God's people are to live as "light" and "salt," according to the teaching of Jesus. This certainly does not mean that the explicit affirmation and pursuit of biblical wisdom makes it automatic or assured. As Chi points out, by their very nature, confession, repentance, and lament are practices that urge a wisdom that humbly faces our failure to seek or to practice the wisdom of God in our private and public lives and yet moves forward with honesty and hope.

Across all of these dimensions of life, wisdom is needed and available, a lifeline in life and in death. It is not a "key" but a "way" to better living. Wisdom brings its benefits and costs. Humility, self-sacrifice, service toward others, and releasing some of the tools and instincts of power are all costly acts that embody being wise. Wisdom is about the long game more than the short game. Self-regulation for the well-being of the other or of the whole is necessary. It is as much about absorbing as it is about propelling, though both are valid. The wise leader inspires and equips rather than demands and subordinates.

If you are seeking wisdom, don't rush reading this book. Savor it. Reread each chapter two or three times. Write about the thoughts and actions it stimulates and the questions it raises. Share this experience with others on the road of life with you—at work, at home, at school, at church, or wherever. Allow it to steep and to lead you into life—abundant life. Chi is such a valuable guide or witness to this wisdom that can animate life in every dimension, honoring the real you and releasing you from the self-centered and self-curated life on sale every day. Choose wisdom and find life. Truly.

MARK LABBERTON, PhD
President Emeritus
Fuller Theological Seminary
Pasadena, Phoenix, and Houston

Acknowledgments

I have to admit that I expected the journey of being an author to be a solitary one. But to my surprise, I discovered that writing is really a communal endeavor, like wisdom itself. So, I want to acknowledge my many companions on the way to completing this book.

Mark Roberts deserves particular note since he was one of the earliest encouragers of my "Third Third" vocation as a writer. Thanks, Mark, for seeing that in me and giving me a chance to hone my craft writing for Fuller Theological Seminary's *Life for Leaders*.

Along the same vein, I want to thank Michaela O'Donnell and her colleagues at Fuller for their encouragement and enthusiasm for my book and, even more so, for making wisdom a central emphasis for the De Pree Center's work of serving leaders into the future.

I also want to thank Steve Garber and Jeff Greenman for inviting Alec Hill and me to teach a course entitled "The Wise Leader" for Regent College, Vancouver, and its MA program in Leadership, Theology, and Society. In addition to providing a great title for this book, the course also gave me the perfect context in which to develop the ideas that came to fruition in this book. And special thanks to my teaching partner, Alec Hill, for the joy of teaching together these last four years. I am especially grateful for his keen mind, warm heart, and enthusiastic suggestions on the first draft of this book. Thanks also to the most recent Wise Leader class for their careful reading of and encouraging feedback on my draft manuscript.

A number of other people also gave unstintingly of their time to read and provide insightful comments on early drafts of this book. Among them, I want to acknowledge Laurie Semke, Rebecha Cusack, Michaela O'Donnell, Rod Wilson, Mark Roberts, Steve Garber, Steve Bell, Chris Lowney, Matthew Kaemingk, Jeff Van Duzer, Al Erisman, and Jody Vanderwel.

My thanks also go to my agent, Don Pape, for his passionate representation of and advocacy for this book. And I am grateful to James Earnest, editor in chief of William B. Eerdmans Publishing Company, for his belief in this book, and to his team for their enthusiastic support in getting this book to publication.

A number of friends prayed faithfully for my writing project. These included Don Waite, Laurie and Rob Semke, Dianne and Roger Morton, Larry and Linda Williams, Larry and Lorann Bjork, Joe and Linda Peritore, Bruce and Chris MacRae, Rebecha and Ken Cusack, and Russ and Sue Goodman. As the poet George Herbert wrote, prayer is "reversed thunder." I cannot imagine writing this book without your prayerful companionship and support along the way.

This book is the work of a lifetime. Along the way, I've had the privilege of knowing and working with many extraordinary people, including those in for-profit businesses, nonprofit organizations, and faith-based institutions. And I've had the privilege of being part of and growing up in a multicultural family that has a rich and diverse set of wisdom traditions. Thanks to each and to all of you who have contributed to what wisdom I have learned along the way.

Finally, my most important thanks go to my wife, Gayle, without whom this book would never have been written. Your life makes my life possible. And I hope the reverse is also true. But I suspect I got the better end of that deal.

June 2023

Introduction

I don't usually save birthday cards. But I recently received a keeper from my forty-something son, Peter. The caption read: *The older I become, the wiser you get.*

Isn't that how it is! Wisdom seems to correlate with age. If not with the age of the person who is deemed wise, then at least with the age and in the eyes of the beholder.

When I was a young boy, my grandfather, Qi Rushan, struck me as a wise man. He wore the robe of a Chinese scholar, so there was a Yoda-like quality about his appearance. And he spoke words that were measured and seemed wise, even to someone very young. I suppose it didn't hurt that everyone I knew—both family and friends— treated him with great respect, even reverence.

I learned later in life that he was remarkably accomplished. It would be tempting to call him a Renaissance man except for the apparent cultural dissonance. He was a respected academic who studied and wrote about Chinese opera as an art form. But he was no mere theoretician. He also wrote Chinese operas and was involved in their performance. And he traveled internationally, promoting Chinese opera to other cultures.[1]

---

1. "Qi Rushan," *Encyclopedia Britannica*, accessed June 7, 2023, https://www .britannica.com/biography/Qi-Rushan.

His interests not only spanned the arts but spread to commercial ventures as well. He and two of his brothers worked in a family-owned store in Beijing early in the twentieth century. And his family was involved in starting a soybean business in France.

His international work was surprising at a time when China was more inwardly focused. But my grandfather was unexpectedly outward looking. He advocated engaging the Western world when that was culturally unpopular in China. He even helped develop a work-study program for promising Chinese students in France.

Of course, I knew little of these accomplishments when I was a child. I simply knew him as my grandfather. As I've thought about what it means to be a wise leader, this picture of my grandfather has come repeatedly to mind. The photo was taken when my grandfather took me for a walk in his garden. This picture is suggestive because it illustrates five things I learned from him about wisdom.

First of all, wisdom is *gracious* and *hospitable*. As the picture intimates, my grandfather delighted in showing me his world. Even as a child, I was invited into the beautiful garden that surrounded his home. I found out early on that wisdom is learned in the presence of gracious and hospitable hosts who are willing to welcome one into the spaces and places they love.

And so, second, wisdom itself is an *expression of love*. Among many other things, my grandfather loved his garden. And he loved to share what he loved with those he loved. Of course, I couldn't begin to understand all that he knew. But I saw that he loved what he knew. I learned that wisdom knows what it knows because it loves its subject. And I also learned that wisdom loves those who want to know what it loves.

Third, wisdom is not self-absorbed but is *focused on the other*. In the picture, my grandfather pointed to something in his garden. His attention was on what was outside of himself, not on himself. Wisdom is neither about us nor about how wise we are.

Fourth, wisdom *empowers the other*. As the picture suggests, my grandfather didn't practice wisdom by sitting me down for a lecture about his garden. Wisdom isn't merely about communicating

My grandfather, Qi Rushan

information or demonstrating cleverness. Instead, he took me into his garden and allowed me to explore that garden for myself. I experienced his love for his world and the world that he loved. I came to know at a young age that wisdom is learned in practice. Wisdom is a matter not only of the head but also of the heart and the hands.

Finally, wisdom *generates delight*. In this picture, my grandfather, perhaps reflecting his natural reserve, showed only a sliver of a smile. But you can't miss the delight on my face. Perhaps my most enduring childhood memory of wisdom is that it resulted in a palpable and playful joy.

Wisdom is a gracious and hospitable host. Wisdom is an expression of love both for its subject and its recipient. Wisdom is more concerned about the other than about itself. Wisdom empowers others to experience for themselves the world that the wise person loves. And wisdom ultimately results in joy and delight in its beneficiary. Those are some of the insights I learned from my grandfather.

The poet T. S. Eliot once wrote, "In my beginning is my end."[2] Unknown to me at the time, my grandfather set me off on a life of seeking after the kind of wisdom he seemed to embody. Perhaps it's no surprise that I find myself writing a book, toward the end of my life, about what it means to live and lead wisely.

SOME ORIENTATION FOR MY READERS

This book is, in many ways, a memoir, a collection of reflections and stories of my journey on the path of wisdom. One of my experiences of wisdom is that it brings together surprising and seemingly unrelated things. So, in addition to personal stories and reflections, you will find discussions of art, literature, and poetry interspersed in this book. My hope is that you find these not as mere curiosities but as material contributions to your experience of reading this book. (To that end, I've included links to a website where you can find all the art referenced in this book.)

Another aspect that may surprise some is my focus on the biblical tradition of wisdom. Recent research on wisdom, particularly as a leadership category, has focused on contributions from Eastern traditions, classical philosophy, and modern science.[3] Without a doubt, as

---

2. T. S. Eliot, "East Coker," in *The Complete Poems and Plays, 1909–1950* (New York: Harcourt Brace, 1980), 123.

3. See, for example, Robert J. Sternberg and Judith Gluck, eds., *The Cam-*

I will argue in chapter 2, there is much to be learned from all of these, as the above story about my grandfather illustrates. But surprisingly, we have neglected the long and rich cultural inheritance from the biblical tradition. In many ways, writing this book has been for me like rediscovering a priceless Van Gogh painting long forgotten in our cultural attic. It would be an incalculable loss to ignore.

Consequently, you will find considerable references to the Hebrew and Christian Bibles in my reflections. For those unfamiliar with those traditions, I hope the references encourage you to see for yourself what those ancient texts might say to us in the twenty-first century. For those who are familiar, I hope my reflections cause you to take another, fresh look at them, particularly as it relates to the question of what it means to live and lead wisely today.

It's my conviction that wisdom is essential for leadership. It doesn't take much to find current, and sometimes spectacular, examples of bad leadership. Sadly, in both the secular and religious spheres, folly abounds. It would be easy to despair. But ancient voices offer us hope. As the Hebrew prophet Jeremiah said millennia ago in similarly discouraging and even dire times:

> Stand at the crossroads, and look,
>   and ask for the ancient paths,
>   where the good way lies; and walk in it. (Jer. 6:16)

To put the challenge in contemporary terms, as voiced in the movie trilogy *The Lord of the Rings*: "Some things that should not have been forgotten were lost."[4]

My hope is that this book is a small contribution to the re-

---

bridge Handbook of Wisdom (Cambridge: Cambridge University Press, 2019), and Ikujiro Nonaka and Hirotaka Takeuchi, "The Big Idea: The Wise Leader," *Harvard Business Review*, May 2011, https://hbr.org/2011/05/the-big-idea-the -wise-leader.

4. From the introduction to the first film, *The Fellowship of the Ring*.

covery of what has been neglected, if not lost altogether, in the twenty-first century.

A Quick Overview of the Book

Chapters 1 and 2 explore key insights about wisdom from biblical perspectives and how those insights interact with other cultures and traditions. Despite their claim to divine origins, one of the surprising aspects of Jewish and Christian wisdom traditions is their core focus on humility rather than hubris. This leads naturally to the question of how to apply that kind of wisdom to leadership, in particular in the exercise of humility and power, which are explored in chapters 3 to 5. Again, perhaps surprisingly, such wisdom sees humility and power not as incompatible opposites but as two sides of the same leadership coin. Humility is not the renunciation of power, but power must always be exercised with humility. Next, chapters 6 and 7 focus on key elements of shaping wisdom in leaders: the development of a countercultural way of life and of seeing the world, through the formation of a leader's character and vision. Finally, chapter 8 provides a multifaceted understanding of wisdom as a lifelong journey.

I hope that you will find this book intriguing and helpful on your journey. And I hope that the joy and delight that wisdom evoked in me as a child—and continues to evoke in my old age—will be yours as you reflect on what I have written.

I

Wisdom from Above

Iam a mathematician by disposition and training. Mathematics and the physical sciences have fascinated me since childhood. In my teens, I wanted to be a theoretical physicist because I wanted to understand the universe's inner workings.

Mathematics was (and is) attractive to me because of its beauty and reliability. It provides an elegant way to describe how the universe works in a small amount of mental space. And it is reliable in the sense that its truth doesn't depend on how anyone feels about it or even whether anyone believes it to be true. For example, the area of a circle is pi times the radius squared. It doesn't matter whether you believe it, or whether on any given day you feel that it is true or not. It just is.

Further, mathematics doesn't merely describe simple things, such as the area of a circle. It describes how much of the complex physical world works. One of the significant contributions of science in the last few centuries has been using mathematics to explain complex physical phenomena accurately.

The explanatory power of mathematics made it plausible for me and many others to think that the universe might be describable by and in that sense reducible to a set of propositions about it. That idea captivated me, and I spent a good deal of my early life pursuing mathematics and science as a way to understand truth and wisdom that is universal.

But my pursuit led me to a conundrum. If it is possible to describe all of reality as a set of impersonal and purposeless forces, why is that possibility so deeply dissatisfying to me as a human being? Being intellectually honest, I had to admit that it is possible "that's just the way reality is." But, for the same reason, I had to also acknowledge the possibility that the human longing for transcendent meaning and purpose suggests something more.

It *is* remarkable that human beings can accurately understand the universe's inner workings. It is equally remarkable that we have a longing to understand the meaning and purpose of that universe. It seems very odd for human beings to have such a deeply ingrained desire for meaning and purpose if there is no such meaning and purpose to be found. Perhaps that's just the way it is. But perhaps not.

Perhaps humanity is meant not just to understand how the universe works but also to understand why the universe exists. What if humanity's purpose is to articulate both the insights of science about the intricacies of the universe and the wisdom of the meaning and purpose of that universe and its Creator?

That question brings me to what I want to explore in this book. This book is a culmination of my lifelong journey, beginning with my love for mathematics and science, leading to a longing for meaning that found its fulfillment in the biblical faith and its embodiment of "the wisdom from above."

THE WAY OF WISDOM

We live in a world filled with information. More than any other generation in history, people today are awash with new knowledge. Simply learning to cope with the resultant mental overload has become a necessary skill for living. What are we to do with all this information? What is essential for me to know? How do we make sense of what it means? How should I live as a result? These are questions that perplex us all. These are also questions about wisdom.

The accumulation of wisdom and the accumulation of knowledge are not the same thing. So, how does one begin if one wants to be wise, particularly now?

Jewish and Christian tradition provides a simple, if startling, answer: "The fear of the LORD is the beginning of wisdom" (Ps. 111:10).

That is a shocker in a world that regularly acts like God doesn't exist. Simply seeking to know more and more, either as individuals or as a society, is no guarantee of becoming wise. If we take that ancient counsel seriously, it seems we must start at a different place.

So, what might it mean to "fear the Lord"? And why is that the starting point in our journey to becoming wise?

Fear is a natural human response to what is unknown and perhaps dangerous. We naturally fear forces that are out of our control, which may turn out to be malevolent. The remarkable scientific discoveries of the last few centuries describe a physical universe that is far greater, far older, and far more complex than any of our forebears could have imagined. Suppose this remarkable universe was not just the result of random, impersonal forces. In that case, more than any who preceded us, our generation should be eager to understand the purpose of the One who created it. Indeed, taking that search seriously is part of what it means to fear the Lord.

Sadly, the very success of the scientific method has made that search more difficult. Some have argued that all knowledge must be subject to the scientific method. Everything true must be verifiable empirically.

The problem with that argument is that, according to the biblical witness, the Creator of the physical universe exists distinct from the physical universe. Unlike the universe, God is not subject to scientific experimentation. Another way of knowing is required. That way of knowing is also part of what it means to fear the Lord.

The good news of the biblical witness is that the God who made all things visible and invisible is neither capricious nor malevolent.

The LORD is good to all,
   and his compassion is over all that he has made.
   (Ps. 145:9)

And while not examinable in a laboratory, God has gone to great
lengths, particularly by the revelation to Moses on Mount Sinai, in
the person of Jesus of Nazareth, and through the availability of God's
Spirit, to be accessible to human beings.

But the nature of wisdom is that it must be sought. Like scientific
discovery, human engagement is essential. Wisdom is not acquired
passively. Wisdom requires personal vulnerability and risk because
it is about a relationship with another person. That, too, is part of
what it means to fear the Lord.

So, if this fear of the Lord leads to wisdom, what might that wisdom look like?

WISDOM IS ABOUT A PERSON

One of the fundamental claims of the biblical tradition is that God
is a person. If that claim is valid, behind the visible universe is not
just a set of impersonal forces but someone who created with intention and meaning. And that would mean that reality is more than a
universe describable with mathematical abstractions and the scientific method, as useful as they are. If God is a person, then the ultimate questions of reality are not "What?" or "How?" but "Who?"
and "Why?"

The Roman governor Pilate, who interrogated Jesus before his
crucifixion, asked, "What is truth?" (John 18:38). From the same gospel account, we learn that Jesus had previously told his followers that
he was "the way, and the truth, and the life" (John 14:6). In asking his
question, Pilate committed what some call a category mistake. Truth
is ultimately found not in an impersonal set of ideas but in a person.
Interestingly, Pilate made that mistake despite Jesus standing right
before him. And Pilate is not alone.

Perhaps a personal illustration would be helpful. I have been married to my wife, Gayle, for a long time. Over the years, I have come to love her deeply and know her well. I have also developed some ideas about what is "true" about her. Invariably, however, she surprises me. Sometimes that can be delightful. At other times, it can be less so. Gayle, at times, perplexes and frustrates me, when she acts differently than what I think is "true" about her (in fairness, I know the reverse is also true!). That is the nature of dealing with real persons, not just mental abstractions.

In a profound sense, I cannot control, or even manage, Gayle. That's a disturbing discovery for someone like me, who likes to be in control and whose professional life is about delivering expected results through other people. But it also leads me to develop a certain respect for our relationship as partners in life. There is a bit of "fear" involved since our relationship is based on my being vulnerable and at risk (of course, again, the reverse is also true for her).

I find that illustration helpful as a metaphor for our relationship with God. If my relationship with Gayle is based on healthy respect, awe, and even "fear," how much more is that an appropriate posture for our relationship with the God of the universe? It should not be surprising the ancients counsel us that "the fear of the LORD is the beginning of wisdom."

But for a host of reasons, the word "fear" is problematic. For one, there is the power dynamic between God and human beings. God is, after all, the Creator of all things, and we are mere and, in many ways, insignificant creatures. There are countless stories in both religious and secular history where such a power differential has been abused with tragic, even horrific, consequences. How can we be sure that God isn't like that?

I offer three reflections that have been helpful to me.

First, the biblical account demonstrates that *God has a deep, personal concern for* and commitment to *those without power*— particularly those who live on the margins of society. Rather than being preoccupied only with the rich and powerful, God is concerned about the poor and the weak.

To the astonishment of his generation, the prophet Isaiah declared of the Creator of the universe: "I dwell on high . . . with the crushed and low in spirit."[1] No wonder Jesus, who Christians believe is God come as a human being,[2] demonstrates the same focus in his life and work. As Jesus famously said: "Come to me, all you that are weary and are carrying heavy burdens, and I will give you rest. Take my yoke upon you, and learn from me; for I am gentle and humble in heart, and you will find rest for your souls. For my yoke is easy, and my burden is light" (Matt. 11:28–30).

Second, it is instructive to see how God acts under the pressure of a relational crisis. As many of us know, a person's character is best seen in the crucible of difficult circumstances. And there are few circumstances more difficult than dealing with a deeply personal conflict.

Early in God's history with the nation of Israel, Israel committed its first great sin of idolatry. While waiting for Moses to come down from Mount Sinai, the people became impatient and asked Moses's brother, Aaron, to make an idol of a golden calf.[3] We in the developed world of the twenty-first century find it hard to relate to the significance of that event. Few of us practice worshiping physical idols. A helpful, if graphic, analogy may be to imagine being newly married and discovering our spouse having sex with a stranger on our honeymoon. That striking parallel captures the horror of Israel's action at the base of Mount Sinai. And so the question became, what would God do next?

An interchange followed between God and Moses to see whether the relationship between God and Israel could be salvaged. Most striking about that conversation is God's self-disclosure at the end: "The LORD, the LORD, the compassionate and gracious God, slow to anger, abounding in love and faithfulness" (Exod. 34:6 NIV).

---

1. Isa. 57:15, trans. John Goldingay, *The First Testament: A New Translation* (Downers Grove, IL: IVP Academic, 2018).

2. For an artistic portrayal, see Rembrandt van Rijn, *Head of Christ*, 1640, at https://depree.org/wise-leader/image-1.

3. That story is found in Exod. 32–34.

Relational catastrophe became an opportunity to demonstrate God's character. Paradoxically, Israel's first significant failure shines a bright light on God's essential nature. So striking and unexpected was this response that this self-disclosure became Israel's catchphrase throughout its history for what their God is like. God's self-description became embedded in their collective memory and regularly reappeared in Israel's prayers, praises, and prophetic teachings.[4]

Finally, Jesus exhibits the full force of God's character in his life and death. Any doubt about how God feels about and acts toward his creatures is dispelled by the most well-known verse in the Christian Bible: "For God so loved the world that he gave his only Son, so that everyone who believes in him may not perish but may have eternal life" (John 3:16).

And to clarify what that means in terms of God's use of power (if Jesus's death on our behalf is not enough), we have God's word to the apostle Paul, *"My power is made perfect in weakness"* (2 Cor. 12:9). I will say more about power later, but for now, that's a good reminder that God's use of power is radically different from what we as human beings fear and what we often experience—power as malevolent violence.

As all this suggests, the wisdom from above embodied in the person of Jesus is profoundly countercultural and counterintuitive. It inverts our expectations of what it means to be wise and to live wisely. What that suggests to me is that wisdom doesn't come naturally to us as human beings. We must both unlearn and relearn what it means to be wise. That, too, is part of what it means to fear the Lord.

WISDOM IS ROOTED IN COMMUNITY

The Christian vision of the wisdom from above involves not only a person but a relationship with a community of persons. As Andrei

---

4. See, for example, Neh. 9:17; Pss. 86:15; 103:8; 145:8; Joel 2:13; Jonah 4:2.

Rublev's ancient icon *The Trinity*[5] wonderfully illustrates, mutuality between persons is at the heart of the universe.

Understanding God as a community of persons lets us see that becoming wise means we are neither merely students coming to get wisdom from a divine teacher nor mystics seeking union with the divine essence. We are not just seeking sacred information or divine absorption.

Unexpectedly, we are invited as persons into a community of persons, the fellowship of the Trinity. As the early apostolic witness confirms: "We declare to you what we have seen and heard so that you also may have fellowship with us; and truly our fellowship is with the Father and with his Son Jesus Christ" (1 John 1:3).

Community is at the heart of wisdom. What might that mean for us?

For one, it helps us understand why reconciliation is such a central theme of wisdom. Ensuring flourishing relationships, including mending broken ones, is core to wise living. Being human means a lifelong journey of cultivating and sustaining healthy relationships.

But if healthy relationships are critical, we must *focus on the well-being of others without ignoring our own*. If mutual flourishing is the goal, we must practice both self-care and care for one another. Self-denial may be a Christian virtue, but self-neglect is not. Being invited into the divine fellowship implies a profound dignity for the human person. So, the wisdom from above requires us to navigate the twin dangers of narcissism and self-neglect.[6]

The apostle Paul threads the needle in just this way, with his counsel in one of his earliest letters to the Christians in Galatia. Paul's Galatian disciples were instructed to "bear one another's burdens" while

5. Andrei Rublev, *The Trinity*, c. 1400, available at https://depree.org/wise-leader/image-2.

6. For an excellent treatment on this subject, see Julie Canlis, "Self-Care Only Works in God's Care," *Christianity Today*, March 10, 2022, https://www.christianitytoday.com/ct/2022/march-web-only/lent-self-care-discipline-discipleship-works-gods-care.html.

they "carry their own loads" (Gal. 6:2, 5). The needs surrounding us can easily overwhelm our capacity to care for ourselves. Wisdom learns to discern what is ours to carry, not only for our sake but also for the sake of others.

Further, wisdom's focus on relationships reminds us to *care for the wider community*, including those beyond our immediate circle of concern. We are called to care for people who are not immediately or directly connected to us. The wisdom from above requires us to develop a culture of hospitality toward those different from us, particularly with whom we would not naturally associate. We need to see those who seem alien as God's gifts, providential neighbors rather than random enemies. Gratitude for and generosity toward outsiders mark those on the way of wisdom.

Finally, wisdom's focus on relationships challenges us to be prepared, when necessary, to *sacrifice for others*. God has supremely demonstrated that in the person of Jesus, "reconciling the world to himself" (2 Cor. 5:19). Like Jesus, we are called to go first where no one else wants to go. Mending relationships is hard. Taking the initiative to do so is even harder. When injuries are deep, it takes considerable discernment to know what needs to be done. Sometimes, it takes a long time.

I had a falling out with a close friend a long time ago. Feeling betrayed by his actions, I suffered profound personal and professional ramifications from the breach. To be fair, he felt the same way. We tried to resolve our differences with the help of a third party, but the relationship seemed irretrievably broken. For a long time, I felt deeply troubled by my inability—or was it my unwillingness?—to fix the relationship.

Almost a decade later, after a near-death experience, my friend initiated a reconciling conversation with me. It was an extraordinary act of humility and grace on his part, and it allowed each of us to own his part in the conflict.

My friend sacrificed his ego and pride to reach out to me. It took a near-death experience for him to do so. His ability to respond to

God's gracious work of reconciliation allowed us to put things right
with one another before he died. His act humbled me and has taught
me something essential about the challenge of serving a relationship.
It's costly to go first.

WISDOM CARES ABOUT EMBODIMENT

I love Caravaggio's painting *Adoration of the Shepherds*.[7] The medie-
val artist imaginatively captures the down-to-earth realism of Jesus's
birth. It's easy to romanticize and spiritualize the process of God becoming a human being. Caravaggio reminds us that it was a difficult
and dirty business. Mary's exhaustion, Joseph's anxious concern for
his young wife and newborn child, and the reality of giving birth in
a working stable with animal excrement seem an unlikely context for
God's grand entrance into the world.

But, as John's Gospel reminds us, "The Word became flesh and
lived among us" (John 1:14). And that means that God became a real
person in real history. Among many other things, that also means
that God cares deeply about the contexts and particularities of our
lives. God became one of us.

The wisdom from above is concerned about flesh-and-blood
people. Wisdom cares about real, embodied existence. It deals with
particular lived experiences, not just a set of ideas or ideals. Several
consequences flow out of that insight.

To begin with, *context and details* are essential. If that's the case,
then one of wisdom's key attributes is the ability to watch and listen
carefully. I tend to think of myself as a pretty good observer and
listener. I try to pay close attention to what others are saying with
their nonverbal cues. But every so often, I get caught up short.

More often than I care to admit, my wife, Gayle, says to me, "You
haven't heard a word I said!" And she's usually right. I've already

---

7. Caravaggio, *Adoration of the Shepherds*, 1609, available at https://depree
.org/wise-leader/image-3.

mentally concluded what I "know" she is trying to say, or I've become preoccupied with what I'm going to say next. As a result, I stop paying attention to our actual conversation.

Further, *nuance and complexity* matter. For better or worse, human beings are complicated, and no amount of wishing makes them otherwise. Said more positively, the human adventure is rich precisely because of our capacity for nuance and complexity. Whenever those are lost, we become caricatures of our intended humanity.

My mother recently passed away at the age of 100. She had prepared careful instructions, also known as health-care directives, for what she did and didn't want done at the end of her life. As someone long associated with health-care systems, I'm a big believer in providing clear guidance for one's medical team and family about one's health-care wishes at the end of life.

Nevertheless, even with such clear instructions, I was surprised by how complex and nuanced those decisions became. In her case, she had to deal with a broken hip, the option of surgery and rehab, pain management, and hospice care. It would have been impossible to describe ahead of time how she wanted her medical team to respond to each of the circumstances she encountered. As helpful as her written instructions were, she needed to have someone she trusted and who loved her at her side to help her navigate the complex challenges of dying. Wisdom for her required a person to address the particulars of her end-of-life experience.

Finally, *mystery and paradox* are inherent to the wisdom from above. As I suggested earlier, dealing with real persons involves not knowing what they will do ahead of time. There is a mystery in relating to another, especially when the other is the Creator of the universe! But not knowing needn't be dreadful. It can also be delightful. There can be a playfulness to not knowing.

There are a couple of early accounts of Jesus's resurrection where we see such an interplay between Jesus and his disciples. One is Jesus's encounter with Mary Magdalene on Easter morning, where Mary mistook Jesus for a gardener (John 20:11–18). The other is Jesus joining some disciples, who mistook him for a stranger, on their walk to the village of Emmaus (Luke 24:13–35).

In both cases, Jesus plays with his disciples. We don't often think of Jesus (or God!) being playful, but that's what these stories describe. It's easy to miss the delightful and even amusing lightheartedness in the mystery of the disciples' encounters with Jesus, as it is with our own. We will explore playfulness as a dimension of wisdom in chapter 8.

It is also easy to dismiss the paradoxes that we encounter in our journey of wisdom. But wisdom sometimes exhibits itself in contradictory ways. Take, for example, the advice from the sage of Proverbs:

> Do not answer fools according to their folly,
>   or you will be a fool yourself.
> Answer fools according to their folly,
>   or they will be wise in their own eyes. (Prov. 26:4–5)

So, which is the wise thing to do? The answer appears to be both—even though the advice is contradictory. The Old Testament scholar Tremper Longman III helpfully suggests that this is an example of where wisdom needs to read what is appropriate for a particular situation.[8] In different circumstances, wisdom suggests different and seemingly contradictory responses.

In an age where knowledge and certainty are highly prized, it is difficult to hold on to mystery and paradox as markers of wisdom. We want to resolve every ambiguity and reconcile every contradiction. But our ancient guides suggest that is unwise. We are not the final arbiters of what is wise. The very presence of mystery and paradox should evoke wonder in us. In that sense too, the fear of the Lord is the beginning of wisdom.

8. Tremper Longman III, *Proverbs* (Grand Rapids: Baker Academic, 2006), 464.

WISDOM EXHIBITS ITSELF IN DIVERSITY

The gift of the Spirit at Pentecost[9] suggests that the wisdom from above is found in a diverse community, not in any individual alone.[10] And that means, in particular, that wisdom is *found in communal discernment*, not merely by an individual on his or her own. That goes against the grain of our highly individualistic culture, where people are expected to know—or at least figure out by themselves—what is the right thing to do.

My experience after I retired from running my software company is a good example. When I retired, friends at a local Christian university asked me to apply for the executive director position at its Center for Integrity in Business. I was honored to be asked and said I wanted some time to consider the matter further.

While I've always appreciated others' input during critical decision-making times, I've tended to be somewhat haphazard in asking for feedback. This time, I decided to be more systematic. I asked thirty people I trusted, who knew me in different contexts, to consider whether the role was right for me.

After giving them time to reflect, I gathered their input. The vast majority of responses were unsurprising. Almost everyone knew of my lifelong interest in working on the intersection of faith and business, which was central to the mission of the Center. Further, the Center had done seminal work articulating a Christian vision of business and had created a considerable following. Finally, the provost was a good friend and strong encourager of my candidacy. Missional alignment, institutional momentum, and senior leadership support—what more could one want as a new leader? As my daughter, Charissa, said a bit tongue in cheek, "What's there to pray about?!"

9. See the story in Acts 2.
10. For a visual representation of the Pentecost event, see the painting by Juan Bautista Maino, *Pentecostés*, c. 1620, available at https://depree.org/wise -leader/image-4.

But two people had different responses. They acknowledged what others had said but asked me to consider whether the position fit what I wanted to do in this new season of life. Both independently suggested that building and leading the Center's program—similar to leadership work I had done in my professional life—would conflict with my expressed desire to teach and write. In their view, the latter was something new that needed deliberate attention and cultivation. And while the former would come more naturally to me, it would consume most, if not all, of my attention and energy. Their insights were surprising but spot-on. And it resulted in me withdrawing my candidacy.

That experience taught me the value of communal discernment and the importance of engaging with diverse perspectives. And it taught me the value and importance of listening to minority voices. The minority is not always correct, of course. But then, neither is the majority, as my experience demonstrated.

The wisdom from above suggests that human beings need communities that are broadly diverse yet profoundly united. Iain Provan, an Old Testament scholar, argues that the Hebrew word (*kenegdo*) used to describe the relationship between Adam and Eve in the creation story means "*like* [but] *opposite.*"[11] That's a terrific insight.

I've spoken before of my long relationship with my wife, Gayle. Provan's phrase is an apt description of the two of us. When we became empty nesters, Gayle and I asked a good friend, who was a trained psychologist, to help us navigate our new season of life. She suggested that Gayle and I take the latest psychological instrument to get a baseline of our personalities. After taking the test, she sat down with us at our living-room coffee table to discuss the results. She looked at us, smiled, and said, "I'm amazed you two are still married!" We were at polar opposite ends in almost every dimension the test measured. We were "opposite" indeed!

11. Iain Provan, *Seriously Dangerous Religion: What the Old Testament Really Says and Why It Matters* (Waco, TX: Baylor University Press, 2014), 87 (quoting Gen. 2:18, emphasis added).

But "like" too. Like many other couples, we were initially attracted to each other by things we recognized in the other—shared interests, values, hopes, and dreams.

Still, if I am honest, I also saw the differences: her focus on the practical and my love of ideas; her love of solitude and my love of gathering people; her critical realism and my unbridled optimism. And the differences I saw in her I often framed as weaknesses in contrast to my strengths. I rarely saw her differences as strengths for my shortcomings. And that was a mistake that's taking me a lifetime to correct.

It has also taken me a long time to appreciate the importance of building a team of "like but opposite" members at work. It is easier to attract and retain people like me, who think as I think and see the world as I do. It's much more challenging to create leadership space for those who differ from me. Not that I am interested in difference for its own sake. There has to be a shared commitment to the vision of the work and the values by which we engage in that work.

Finally, wisdom benefits from *long-term committed relationships*. It helps to have people around who've known you for a long time. In our transient and mobile culture, that's not easy to come by. But it's essential. As we grow in our work and responsibilities, something surprising happens. We develop an insularity—something akin to a bubble—that shields us from the truth about ourselves. For many reasons, people around us become reluctant to get in our face. Having people in our lives who knew us when we were younger and foolish instead of older and polished keeps us connected to the interior realities of who we are.

I've had the privilege of living in the same geographic community for most of my adult life. I know that's not the norm, nor does it need to be. Gayle and I have several lifelong friends who don't live near us. One couple, Laurie and Rob Semke, have experienced life quite differently than we have. While we've stayed rooted in the Seattle area all our married life, they've moved often and lived in many parts of the United States, and have spent several years in Ireland. Nevertheless, we share a joint commitment to maintaining and cultivating a connection across time and space. That investment creates a deep reservoir of wisdom to draw on at different times and seasons.

Wherever you find yourself, it is not too late to invest in deeper personal relationships, perhaps rekindling old ones. Even more than building our financial portfolio, building a community of "like but opposite" people around us takes time and effort but provides lasting results. Not least, access to wisdom is one of its fruits.

WISDOM IS DISCOVERED ON A JOURNEY

The final characteristic of the wisdom from above is that it is discovered on a journey that involves trust and vulnerability. And that journey ultimately includes a willingness to suffer loss, as demonstrated vividly by Rembrandt's painting *The Sacrifice of Isaac*.[12]

In that sense, wisdom is risky and expensive. Wisdom is neither inborn nor learned casually. It takes deliberate and difficult choices to form the character of a person who would be wise.

Even though the painting demonstrates Abraham's greatest act of faith and trust in God, that's not how his story began. Abraham's journey reminds us that we only learn by *failing along the way*. Abraham's early experience illustrates the point. Abraham demonstrated questionable morals and faith in Egypt (Gen. 12:10–20) as well as with Hagar and Ishmael (Gen. 16). With Abraham, we discover that the price of learning wisdom is failure.

I took up downhill skiing when I was in my late teens. I had a friend named Jeff who learned to ski along with me. I quickly discovered that we had two very different styles of learning. Mine was to carefully navigate my way down the slope, trying not to fall. Jeff, on the other hand, was a madman. He barreled straight down the hill, falling regularly, and I might add, with great enthusiasm.

---

12. Rembrandt van Rijn, *Sacrifice of Isaac*, c. 1635, available at https://depree .org/wise-leader/image-5.

Guess who learned to ski well? It wasn't me. My tentativeness—at least about skiing—kept me from learning, much less learning quickly. So in the journey of wisdom, being cautious is not always a virtue.

I remember a conversation with my friend and mentor Max De Pree, near the end of his life. We were chatting about some frustrations I had encountered in my business. I told him how difficult it was to have had a string of successes and then to discover, at the peak of my career, that I couldn't help my business reach another level of success. I wondered out loud what I was doing wrong. Max turned to me and said quietly, "Maybe you need to fail at something."

That's the last thing I expected to hear. I was hoping for wisdom on turning things around, or at least identifying what was needed to help the business succeed. Instead, I was given a stark assessment that I had missed the point. Perhaps failure is necessary on the way to wisdom. Perhaps, as the apostle Paul learned centuries ago in his work, God's power really is perfected in weakness. It's a startling lesson to learn at the height of one's professional career. Discovering the limits of our capacities and gifts is a painful thing.

At the same time, another aspect of wisdom is to *persist on the journey in the face of adversity and resistance.* We may fail, but we also need to get up and keep going. Abraham may not always have behaved well, but he continued his faith journey. And he had plenty of obstacles along the way: the long wait for an heir, the infertility of old age, and God's promises that seemed like pipe dreams.

In an age of convenience and quickly acquired knowledge, it's easy to be lulled into a sense that things should be less difficult. Even those trained in the Christian way find that an easy mistake to make.

I had a thoughtful pastoral friend who was struggling with his congregation. At one particularly frustrating point, he said to me in exasperation, "Pastoral ministry shouldn't be this hard!" I turned to him and said, "Whoever gave you that idea?" But I understood what he meant. The struggles of life and work, whether in pastoral ministry or running a technology company, can be wearying. Wisdom's call to persist in adversity is as necessary as it is difficult.

Finally, wisdom is risky and expensive because it invariably brings us to points where we need to *sacrifice with courage*. After waiting all of his life for an heir, Abraham is tested by God (Gen. 22:1), who asks him to sacrifice his son, his only, beloved son, Isaac.[13] Isaac was likely a teenager by this time. Abraham must have watched him grow with the unique joy of having a child in old age, the fulfillment of God's extraordinary promise and of Abraham's persistent faith. And now this.

After all of Abraham's journeys, God asks for his son as a human sacrifice. How is that even possible? That's what those who worship the idols of Canaan do. It's hard to imagine a more inappropriate request and a greater challenge to the foundation of Abraham's faith. Is the God of Abraham really good? Is the God of Abraham capricious like the other gods of the ancient world, promising one thing and then doing something else? Can the God of Abraham be trusted?

Surely, these questions must have been swirling in Abraham's mind as he considered what he would do. And for those familiar with the earlier part of the Genesis story, these questions are eerily reminiscent of the serpent's question in the garden to Abraham's ancestors. The journey of wisdom takes us to strange and unimaginable places.

In a decision that will mark Abraham's life and make it remarkable for all who follow, Abraham chooses to trust in the God he could not comprehend. And he expresses that faith by laying down what is most important to him—the gift God has given him to fulfill his destiny. Abraham offers up Isaac.

In that act, the angel of God says, "Now I know that you fear God" (Gen. 22:12). The fear of the Lord, which is the beginning of wisdom, finds its fulfillment in Abraham. The wisdom that begins in faith ends in faith. Abraham started his journey "not knowing where he was going" (Heb. 11:8). He reached the pinnacle of that journey and then, "when put to the test, offered up Isaac" (Heb. 11:17).

13. I've used this language to mirror the language God used with Abraham, even though everyone knew that Abraham also had another son named Ishmael.

I conclude this chapter with a personal story. I started one of my businesses with a business partner. My partner was a great friend, and we had dreamed about starting a venture together. When the opportunity arose, we discussed how the two of us would make decisions together. We recognized that there would be times when we disagreed and wanted to think through how to resolve those conflicts.

My partner believed it was essential to have a structural way of resolving potential deadlocks. For him, this meant that someone had to have a majority interest, with the other taking a minority position. That way, if we couldn't get to an agreement, the person with majority interest would get to make the decision.

In contrast, I believed that we should share equally in ownership. My view was that if we couldn't agree on an important decision, we had to work through the issues until we did.

He also believed it was appropriate for him to own majority interest. He had more relevant business experience, so it was a reasonable suggestion. We discussed it for a long time, and I finally agreed to both the ownership structure and his holding majority interest.

You might wonder why.

In the middle of that process, I reread the story about Abraham's conflict with his nephew Lot about grazing rights (Gen. 13:1–9). Interestingly, the story concerns the economic flourishing of both Abraham's and Lot's flocks and the resulting competition for land. As the story unfolds, Abraham comes to Lot and says, effectively, "There's plenty of land for the both of us. Let's split up, and if you want to go left, I'll go right. If you're going to go to the right, I'll go to the left. You choose."

I was surprised and challenged by Abraham's faith and example. As the senior member (Abraham was Lot's uncle), he could have easily said, "Listen up, Lot! I'm going to decide what's best for both of us. If I want to go right, you go left. If I want to go left, you go to the right." But he didn't. He deferred to his nephew in a surprising act of humility and gracious use of power. (We'll talk more about both humility and power later.)

That example challenged me to do the same, even though the power dynamics differed. And so, as an act of faith, I agreed to a minority ownership of our business. The surprise that followed was that after about six months, my partner came back to me and suggested we reset our shares of ownership so they would be equal. It was a remarkably gracious act on his part since he wasn't obligated to do so.

Now, I recognize that it didn't have to turn out this way, and I'm not suggesting that it would in other circumstances. But in a small way, my experience reflected what Abraham modeled in his life. While I wasn't asked to give up my only son, there was significant personal sacrifice involved. Those who have started their own business or organization know what it's like to speak of the venture as "your baby." In that sense, I very much felt like I was giving up part of "my baby" and then receiving it back again six months later. It doesn't always happen that way, of course. But I am grateful to God—and to my friend—that it did in this case.

2

Wisdom and the World around Us

Ifirst read *Silent Spring* as a teenager. In her book, Rachel Carson described the long-term environmental effects of the widespread use of pesticides, in particular DDT. It turned out to be a wake-up call to my generation about humanity's destructive effects on our planet. Arguably, the publication of Carson's book became a watershed moment for the modern environmental movement. And despite considerable controversy and opposition, it led to significant policy changes in the United States and internationally, including limiting the use of DDT and related insecticides.

Silent Spring also launched me on a short-lived stint as an environmental activist. I became preoccupied with ecological concerns and began reading books about the human effects on the planet. And I helped organize and lead an ecology club at my local school. I felt like I was doing something to contribute to a better world.

As it happened, around the same time, I had my first encounter with what I described in the last chapter as the wisdom from above. My local public high school offered a course entitled "The Bible as Literature." Having grown up knowing almost nothing about the Bible other than it being one of the foundational texts of Western culture, I was intrigued enough to take the course. I was lucky to have a man named Harry Oldenburger teach it.

Harry was someone who took his faith seriously but himself lightly. He had an infectious smile and an evident love for all his students. Exhibiting an unusual humility, he demonstrated a gracious openness and hospitality toward those who thought and believed differently than he did. I suspect that was one of the reasons he was asked to teach the course.

Harry was not only a gifted teacher of the biblical material, but he modeled how someone who took its claims seriously might live out their convictions. His example significantly influenced my giving the Christian faith a serious look.

About the same time, I started attending an after-school, faith-based student club called Young Life. I wish I could say that I went as a seeker after truth. Instead, I went because I was interested in a girl who sat next to me in algebra class and who invited me to go with her to a meeting. God does work in not-so-mysterious ways! When I got there, I found, to my surprise, that I was captivated by the message of Jesus—a message of the God of the universe coming in human form to bring renewal and restoration to a broken world, myself included. In the words of one of my favorite Young Life songs of that time:

> I am the Light of the World
> You people come and follow me.
> If you follow and love, You'll learn the mystery
> Of what you were meant to do and be. . . .
>
> To free the prisoner from his chains,
> To make the powerful care,
> To rebuild the nations with strength and goodwill,
> To call a man your brother everywhere.[1]

---

1. "I Am the Light of the World," Gospel Music Lyrics, accessed June 9, 2023, http://gospelyrics.blogspot.com/2007/09/i-am-light-of-world.html. Words and music © 1968 by Jim Strathdee, Desert Flower Music. Based on the poem "The Work of Christmas," by Howard Thurman.

That hope of transformation—for a better world and a better self—and the promise of participating in that future were part of what attracted me to the Christian faith.

Looking back on my early experiences, you might think the message of Jesus would have reinforced my interest in environmental concerns. Both were concerned with the flourishing of the created world. But quickly, that common interest began to unravel. Why that happened turns out to be directly relevant to the subject of this chapter.

Once I was exposed to the Christian faith, it didn't take long for me to encounter an alternative "religious wisdom" masquerading as "the wisdom from above." That alternative focused primarily on the spiritual and interior dimensions of human life to the exclusion of the physical and exterior world.

It was an attractive temptation and diversion. As someone who had spent his early life focused on making sense of the physical world, the possibility of exploring a previously unimagined interior world was irresistible. So, instead of a steady diet of books on mathematics and physics, I found myself reading spiritual classics and theological texts. At one level, this new interest and fascination were understandable. After all, I was beginning to discover a new inner dimension of being human. But it turned out to be surprisingly difficult to hold together the spiritual and physical dimensions of life. I was experiencing what my friend Steve Garber calls the challenge of living a "seamless life."[2]

As it turns out, the temptation to focus on the spiritual, to the exclusion of the physical, dimension of life has a long history. Various "wisdom traditions" known as Gnosticism developed in the first century around these diversions and distractions from the wisdom from above. It turned out that I was not the only one overly focused on the spiritual life.

---

2. See Steven Garber, *The Seamless Life: A Tapestry of Love and Learning, Worship and Work* (Downers Grove, IL: InterVarsity Press, 2020).

Sadly for me and my newfound faith, I soon lost interest in environmental matters. Rather than engaging the emerging environmental problems of the day, I became preoccupied with my spiritual development. In the early days of my Bible as literature class with Harry Oldenburger, I had written a paper that looked at the Ten Commandments in light of our stewardship of the planet.

Harry encouraged my attempt and even suggested that I publish the paper. Despite his encouragement, I lost all interest a year or two later. Exploring the implications of my faith for the ecological issues of my generation was no longer on my radar. I had adopted a view expressed in the words of a song from that time:

> This world is not my home, I'm just a passing through
> My treasures are laid up somewhere beyond the blue.[3]

Thankfully, that's not where things remained. Not only for me but also for the wider Christian community, the last few decades have seen a groundswell of interest in bringing the considerable resources of the wisdom from above to bear on the urgent environmental issues of our day. Pope Francis's papal encyclical *Laudato Si'—on Care for Our Common Home* provides just such a comprehensive and compelling framework.

Reading Pope Francis's encyclical, I felt saddened that I had spent much of the early part of my life living in two separate worlds. I had allowed a pseudowisdom to disenfranchise the physical world from the contributions of the spiritual world, and vice versa. Strangely, the effect of this kind of religious wisdom turned out to be similar to what on the surface might look like its diametrical opposite—purely secular wisdom. In the former case, the spiritual world is the only one that matters. In the latter, the spiritual world is an illusion. In either

---

3. A. P. Carter, "I Can't Feel at Home Any More," Hymnary.org, accessed June 9, 2023, https://hymnary.org/text/this_world_is_not_my_home_im_just _a?extended=true.

case, the wisdom from above makes no discernible difference to the world in which we live.

Taking Human Responsibility Seriously

In stark contrast, one of the central insights of the biblical wisdom tradition is that human beings are made in the image of God and therefore have a responsible role in the physical world: "Then God said, 'Let us make humankind in our image, according to our likeness; and let them have dominion . . .'" (Gen. 1:26).

Whatever the word "dominion" means (and we will explore that more in chapters 4 and 5), it implies significant human agency in the created order. At a minimum, having dominion involves human responsibility for and engagement with our world. That's a helpful critique of the pseudowisdom I picked up in my youth that focuses exclusively on spiritual detachment from the world around us. It is also a valuable counter to the nihilism ("Whatever!") and narcissism ("It's all about me!") that pervade much of twenty-first-century culture.

Further, it serves as an excellent corrective to some long-standing Christian wisdom traditions that have an overly deterministic view of God's work in the world. In those traditions, God's work is so dominant that human agency disappears from sight. In contrast, noted Old Testament scholar Walter Brueggemann argues that the biblical witness suggests that "Humans have the primary responsibility for their destiny; they are able to decide responsibly."[4]

Despite their considerable positive contributions, Brueggemann contends that the legacies of Saint Augustine and Martin Luther have left the Christian tradition with an inadequate "theology of [human] responsibility."[5]

The French mathematician and Christian philosopher Blaise Pascal is more helpful. Pascal talks about human beings being given "*the*

---

4. Cited in William A. Dyrness, *The Facts on the Ground: A Wisdom Theology of Culture* (Eugene, OR: Wipf & Stock, 2022), 92.

5. Dyrness, *Facts on the Ground*, 92.

dignity of causality."[6] I think he is on to something important. While Pascal was talking specifically about prayer, his insight applies to the larger landscape of humanity's vocation. In ways that may sometimes be mysterious, human beings have been allowed to make a difference in the world.

The dignity of causality is more than our capacity to voice the needs of our world to God, as important as that is. It extends to every aspect of our role as human beings. In the language of the biblical creation story, human beings are made in the image of God. In other words, we are meant to be living, physical embodiments, both individually and in community, of the invisible God in the world.

This means that we have been given the dual gifts of (1) representing God's character and care to the created world and (2) representing the cares and concerns of that created order (including those of other human beings) to God. It's hard to imagine a greater honor or a more awesome responsibility.

Here the language and imagery of human beings as God's "ambassadors" are helpful, and are picked up by the apostle Paul in his writings (see, e.g., 2 Cor. 5:20 and Eph. 6:20). Ambassadors are given delegated power and responsibility by the government they represent. Their words and actions carry weight precisely because they are seen, rightly or wrongly, as an expression of their government's intentions. And their effect is proportional to the power and authority of their government. What is essential to the role of ambassadors is that they be faithful to the values and policies of their government.

Arguably, the vocation of being human is to be that kind of faithful ambassador for the Creator of the universe to the created order. That's what it means for human beings to be made in the image of God. Interestingly, Paul's word for ambassador also means an "elder statesman."[7] In ancient as in modern times, reliable ambassadors

---

6. Blaise Pascal, *Pascal's Pensees* (New York: E. P. Dutton, 1958), 120 (emphasis added).

7. "Presbeuō," Bible Hub, accessed June 9, 2023, https://biblehub.com /greek/4243.htm.

are often people of age and experience. They demonstrate insight and sound judgment concerning their government's intentions. And they understand and thoughtfully engage the culture of the countries to which they are assigned. In both of those respects, mature wisdom is critical. So it is for us as human beings made in the image of God.

It's worth observing that God has taken extraordinary risks in designating human beings as ambassadors. Imagine a modern superpower's ambassador going rogue, and the chaos and damage that would ensue.

Now imagine someone with the delegated authority and power of the Creator of the universe going rogue. That's a helpful way of seeing the role and effect of human beings in the world. More often than not, God's intended representatives do their own thing rather than embodying God's intentions. The potentially disastrous consequences, as well as the possibility of positively contributing to the flourishing of the world, should motivate each of us to be a wise, faithful ambassador.

The message of the wisdom from above is that human beings are responsible actors in the world. And that means that engaging the world around us is not an option. It is a requirement for each of us. How wisdom does that is the subject of the next section.

Taking the World around Us Seriously

Given the extraordinary claims of Judaism and Christianity—Moses's encounter with God on Mount Sinai and the coming of Jesus of Nazareth as God incarnate—it might be easy to assume that the wisdom from above is to be found only in those religious wisdom traditions. In other words, one might conclude that all the wisdom that matters is resident in a chosen people.

But surprisingly, both Jewish and Christian wisdom traditions suggest otherwise. Both recognize that there is wisdom to be found in other cultures. As Old Testament scholar Tremper Longman observes in his commentary of the book of Proverbs:

When Solomon's wisdom is praised, it is evaluated not in contrast to but in comparison to the wisdom of Egypt and other Near
Eastern traditions:

> God gave Solomon very great wisdom, discernment, and breadth
> of understanding as vast as the sand on the seashore, so that Sol-
> omon's wisdom surpassed the wisdom of all the people of the
> east, and all the wisdom of Egypt. (1 Kings 4:29–30 NRSV)

> Such a statement acknowledges the wisdom of the east and of
> Egypt. Solomon's wisdom is not of a completely different order.
> To praise something by saying it is better than something else is
> to appreciate the latter.[8]

Longman and others have noted that the Bible has instances where
its wisdom strongly resembles ancient Egyptian and Babylonian wisdom traditions.[9] While there is debate about the specifics, there is
general agreement that the biblical wisdom tradition drew on the insights of surrounding cultures. As theologian Bill Dyrness observes:
"In an important sense the wise person, in paying attention to creation, is listening for the voice of God. . . . Israel's sages paid close
attention to the 'voice,' the communicative structure of creation, but
so did the sages in neighboring societies."[10]

Even those who are generally skeptical about human wisdom because of their understanding of the consequences of sin and evil acknowledge that there is wisdom to be learned from the world around
us, including in matters of moral virtue. As sixteenth-century Protes-
tant reformer John Calvin noted, "In every age there have been persons who, guided by nature, have striven toward virtue throughout
life. . . . These examples, accordingly, seem to warn us against adjudging
man's nature wholly corrupted, because some men have by its prompt-

---

8. Tremper Longman III, *Proverbs* (Grand Rapids: Baker Academic, 2006), 42.
9. Longman, *Proverbs*, 42–56.
10. Dyrness, *Facts on the Ground*, 83–84.

ing not only excelled in remarkable deeds, but conducted themselves honorably throughout life. But here it ought to occur to us that amid this corruption of nature there is some place for God's grace."[11]

There is a remarkable interplay in human work and wisdom between God's activity and our own. The wisdom from above teaches that it's not always easy, or perhaps even necessary, for us to sort out which is which. In a beautiful passage in the book of Isaiah, the prophet reflects on the wisdom of God as it relates to the human practice of agriculture:

> Do those who plow for sowing plow continually?
> > Do they continually open and harrow their ground?
> When they have leveled its surface,
> > do they not scatter dill, sow cummin,
> and plant wheat in rows
> > and barley in its proper place,
> > and spelt as the border?
> For they are well instructed;
> > their God teaches them. . . .
> This also comes from the LORD of hosts;
> > he is wonderful in counsel,
> > and excellent in wisdom. (Isa. 28:24–26, 29)

Dyrness then makes this incisive and, for our sake, critical observation:

> But wait, in fact, the farmer did not learn this from God, he learned it from his father, the miller from his mother. But here is the claim: this cumulative human wisdom is also, at the same time, God's. . . . Of course, there was nothing uniquely Jewish about this agricultural wisdom, just as there was nothing Jewish about the [Egyptian] Wisdom of Amenemope that the writer of Proverbs

11. Calvin, quoted in Dyrness, *Facts on the Ground*, 28.

borrowed in Proverbs 22. Its reliability reflected the fact that the wisdom God put in creation worked just as well in Egypt as it did in Israel, because all of it "comes from the Lord."[12]

Practically speaking, this means that the wisdom from above comes not only from receiving "spiritual insight" or "revelation" but also from observation, reflection, and the hard work of study and practice. Both inspiration and perspiration matter in becoming wise. And while we tend to associate the former with God's wisdom and the latter with our own, Dyrness helpfully notes the seamlessness between the two in his concluding reflections on the Isaiah passage: "Though wisdom was human work, the created order, and by extension all that could eventually be made of it, was, at the same time, God's work."[13]

This means that those of us who take seriously the wisdom from above found in our religious traditions need to take with equal seriousness the wisdom that is located in the wider culture. And that's because the wisdom from above is sometimes, if not often, found in the wisdom of our surrounding culture. And that means we need to cultivate an attitude of humility rather than one of hubris about what we know versus what we have to learn from those who may have different convictions than our own. We will further explore the virtue of humility in the next chapter.

For now, it's worth noting that humility and its openness to the perspectives of others don't mean uncritical acceptance of those perspectives. Discernment is a vital aspect of wisdom, never more so than for religious or secular claims to wisdom. We should not be naive about either.

Even further, the wisdom from above recognizes wisdom's own limitations. Dyrness helpfully argues that from the beginning, there is an ambiguous quality to the very notion of being wise: "The use

12. Dyrness, *Facts on the Ground*, 92–93.
13. Dyrness, *Facts on the Ground*, 93.

of wisdom language ('crafty,' 'subtle' KJV) for one of God's creatures, and indeed the appearance of the serpent itself, implies that this temptation, and the evil it entailed, comes from within the goodness of creation, which must have contained this possibility as a condition of its goodness."[14]

Surprisingly then, "The trajectory of death is [also] associated with wisdom, making clear at the earliest stage of human progress that the creative imagination [and wisdom itself] is both gift and problem."[15]

In other words, the very notion of being wise contains the possibility of its misuse, resulting in what Dyrness calls the "trajectory of death." In contrast, the proper use of wisdom results in the "trajectory of life."

Not only can wisdom be misused, but once it is, there's the problem of what to do with the resulting fiasco. How do we deal with the results of pursuing the trajectory of death? There again, wisdom's limitations are clear. There is a difference between the insight that comes from wisdom and the power to deliver from the consequences of its misuse.

As necessary as wisdom is to the work of leadership, it can't and isn't meant to replace God. As we noted above, the fear of the Lord is the beginning and the end of wisdom. In the end, wisdom—at least the wisdom from above that leads to the trajectory of life—brings with it a recognition of humanity's essential and intended relationship with the God in whose image we are all created. And who alone can deliver us from the consequences of the trajectory of death.

Seeing the World Rightly

We live in a media-filled world that seeks our attention. Social media measures its success by the number of eyeballs captured. Attention has become the currency of our digital age. Our attention—or lack thereof—drives advertising, product placement, and even product de-

14. Dyrness, *Facts on the Ground*, 68.
15. Dyrness, *Facts on the Ground*, 69.

sign. Where our eyes go, modern marketing follows. And consequently, modern marketing desires to determine where our eyes should go.

What we pay attention to matters. What we look at—and how we "see" what we look at—shapes who we become. Jesus knew this. As he memorably said in the Sermon on the Mount, "The eye is the lamp of the body. So, if your eye is healthy, your whole body will be full of light; but if your eye is unhealthy, your whole body will be full of darkness. If then the light in you is darkness, how great is the darkness!" (Matt. 6:22–23).

As Jesus taught in that sermon, our "eye," our "heart," and our "treasure" all affect one another. What we focus on, what we desire, and what we value are all deeply interconnected. But our eyes are critical. Our attention requires our attention.

So, to what are we to pay attention? From what Jesus said immediately before his comment about our eyes, it might be easy to conclude that we should focus exclusively on "spiritual matters." That's how many have interpreted Jesus's words, "Do not store up for yourselves treasures on earth . . . but store up for yourselves treasures in heaven" (Matt. 6:19–20).

Perhaps surprisingly, then, Jesus follows these words by directing his followers' eyes not heavenward but earthward: "Look at the birds of the air. . . . Consider the lilies of the field" (Matt. 6:26, 28). Jesus's teaching about the dangers of preoccupation with the material world does not lead to an exclusively heavenly focus. Instead, he directs us to the created, visible world as the place where God's dependable goodness can be seen and learned.

But how we pay attention matters. Jesus's words—"look" and "consider"—are especially important. Neither suggests a casual or an indifferent act. Instead, the first word means to look at something "in a sustained, concentrated way, i.e., with special 'interest, love or concern.'"[16] Perhaps paradoxically, paying that kind of careful attention to the created world is essential to our having "treasures in heaven."

16. "Emblepō," Bible Hub, accessed June 9, 2023, https://biblehub.com/greek/1689.htm.

And the second word Jesus uses ("consider") is an intensified version of a word that means to learn.[17] Learning means looking at something and drawing conclusions from what we see. Looking, even studying the world carefully around us, is not enough. What do we conclude from what we have seen and learned?

Particularly for twenty-first-century readers, Jesus pointedly reminds us that the world is not just the consequence of impersonal forces. The universe and this planet are the handiwork of someone who loves and cares for what has been made. In very practical terms, Jesus directs our attention to the created world—the birds of the air and the lilies of the field—that we might see and learn from them about a compassionate and gracious God who cares for us and the planet we inhabit. Our looking and learning are intended to form a wise imagination about what is going on in the world around us (more on developing that kind of imagination in chapter 7).

But it is possible to draw erroneous conclusions and form the wrong kind of imagination. As I've described in my early experience, in studying the physical world around us—given its ancient history and seemingly reliable physical laws—we might conclude that's all there is to the universe. Similarly, we can look at the cultures around us—both religious and secular—and misinterpret what we must learn from them. Wisdom requires insight and discernment—a wise way of seeing the world—lest the light we gain from the created world and cultures around us turns out to be, in Jesus's words, darkness in us.

How might we tell what is light and what is darkness? How can we distinguish between the "wisdom from above" and what might be called "wisdom from below"?

BEING RIGHTLY IN THE WORLD

According to tradition, Jesus's younger brother is the likely source for the letter from "James" found in the New Testament. If so, the letter

17. "Katamanthanō," Bible Hub, accessed June 9, 2023, https://biblehub.com/greek/2648.htm.

allows us to hear from someone who knew Jesus intimately. James would have seen Jesus in the best and the worst of times. In other words, James had a lifelong, ringside seat to what he would later call "the wisdom from above."

That's why James's description of that wisdom is so interesting. James said this about what he learned from his older brother: "Who is wise and understanding among you? Show by your good life that your works are done with gentleness born of wisdom.... *The wisdom from above* is first pure, then peaceable, gentle, willing to yield, full of mercy and good fruits, without a trace of partiality or hypocrisy. And a harvest of righteousness is sown in peace for those who make peace" (James 3:13, 17–18).

What I find remarkable about what James describes is its focus. For James, the wisdom from above produces a certain kind of person. It's not first and foremost a body of knowledge but rather, as I noted in the last chapter, embodied in a person.

Wisdom is primarily exhibited, to quote Dr. Martin Luther King, by "the content of our character" rather than by what we say and know. To put it negatively, it is possible to know and say the right things and still be the wrong kind of person.

Of course, Jesus knew this. He said much the same at the end of his Sermon on the Mount. He warned that many would claim to speak and act "in his name" and discover that they were wrong. In Jesus's stark and startling words, they will be told, "I never knew you; go away from me, you evildoers" (Matt. 7:23).

So, how do we know whether someone is rightly following the wisdom from above? Jesus gives a simple test: "You will know them by their fruits" (Matt. 7:16). The qualities of our lives are the acid test of whether we are wise or not. That is precisely James's point in his letter. According to James, there is a "wisdom from above" and a "wisdom from below." And the way you tell them apart is by the kind of person and community they produce.

As we seek to wisely engage and learn from the world around us— both religious and secular—this is helpful counsel. Some traditions are helpful; some are not. Jesus's teachings (like James's) suggest that while there is a wisdom from above, work is required to distinguish it from the other kind, "the wisdom from below." And as Jesus warned, that's especially true in religious contexts where people explicitly claim to be acting in God's name.

But it's also true in secular contexts. Secular worldviews of various kinds carry implicit beliefs about the world we inhabit. They are not morally neutral. Even to atheists, some things are good and other things are not. Tolerance is a primal virtue in the secular world, where I spend much of my time. But even tolerance has its limits, if only for the intolerant! Even in a tolerant society, we need wisdom about what should be tolerated and what should not.

My point in all this is that there is much to learn from and guard against in discerning wisdom in the world around us. *Wisdom is about formation, not just about information.* How we engage with the world and learn from the world invariably changes us for better or worse.

The wisdom from above teaches us that we should pay close attention to what is happening inside us and in our communities even as we engage and learn from the religious and secular world around us. What kind of people are we becoming? What types of cultures are we creating in our communities, organizations, and institutions? We will explore these formational aspects of leadership further in chapter 6.

THE POSSIBILITY OF A LASTING LEGACY

When I was ten, I became interested in astronomy. I read books that described the mystery of planets, stars, and galaxies. I learned about the vast reaches of space and the unimaginable period of time that has passed since its beginnings. And I also learned that, at some point, what I saw would come to an end. I'm not sure why, but the thought of the sun burning out, although billions of years in the future, seemed particularly disturbing to me. Perhaps it was its finality—the possibility that everything I knew about family, friends, and maybe all of human history would one day be gone. Never mind that I would not be around to see it. It was a surprisingly depressing thought.

Is this all there is? Perhaps that was the real question behind what was bothering me as a child. Judged on a cosmic timescale, human life doesn't even register as a blip. What are a hundred years on a scale that measures existence in the billions?

And yet . . .

Human beings in most cultures and religious traditions have yearned for a lasting legacy, a life beyond this limited existence. The limits of our physical existence seem to provoke a sadness of unfulfilled potential and a longing for something more. The possibility of "eternal life" has filled the human imagination throughout human history.

Jesus's wisdom from above tells us the possibility of eternal life is not just wishful thinking. In startling terms, Jesus describes the legacy of human beings as extending well beyond this life. That means what we do in this life matters. And not only for this life.

C. S. Lewis imaginatively captures Jesus's teaching in his collection of children's stories entitled The Chronicles of Narnia. In the last book, Lewis describes life in this world as "the cover and the title page . . . of the Great Story, which no one on earth had read: which goes on forever: in which every chapter is better than the one before."[18]

No wonder the apostle Paul, in writing about the implications of Jesus's resurrection for people's lives now, says this: "Therefore, my beloved, be steadfast, immovable, always excelling in the work of the Lord, because you know that in the Lord your labor is not in vain" (1 Cor. 15:58).

But given the realities of our lives and the seeming insignificance of much of our work, how can we imagine our ultimate legacy?

One of Lewis's contemporaries, J. R. R. Tolkien, provides a helpful story that expands my imagination of what our human legacy might

18. C. S. Lewis, *The Last Battle* (New York: Collier Books, 1970), 184.

look like. His short story, "Leaf by Niggle," tells of an insignificant person in a little town who is a painter. The story's main character, a man named Niggle, is working on his "magnum opus," a painting of a particular tree in a specific landscape of his imagination. But despite his best efforts—and perhaps like the experience of many artists—he finds his artistic work frustrated by the interruptions and needs of others as well as his own lack of discipline and diligence. As a result, his great work is left unfinished when he comes to the end of his life.

In Tolkien's imaginative telling, Niggle's death is described as a journey to a different but still recognizably familiar place. To his surprise, what Niggle discovers in that place is not only a recovery of his art but the living tree and landscape of his imagination! His artistic gifts are not only fulfilled but transformed. His unfinished painting is transfigured into a living reality. And again, to his surprise, he is not just a passive observer of this transformation but an active participant in its ongoing creation. Finally, he discovers he is not alone. His formerly bothersome neighbor is there, and Niggle soon finds joy sharing in a new life and work together.

Tolkien's imaginative short story challenges me to see my life in the present differently. His story frames this life as an opportunity to create something of lasting value for the common good, despite our own and others' limitations and failures. And the story suggests that I cannot begin to imagine the final, astonishing result. Tolkien intimates that by finishing what we do not and transforming what we cannot, God's intentions for our legacy are as extraordinary as they are unimaginable. As the apostle Paul said,

> "Eye has not seen, nor ear heard,
> Nor have entered into the heart of man
> The things which God has prepared for those
> who love Him." (1 Cor. 2:9 NKJV)

Not only are our labors not in vain but they will have results beyond our wildest dreams. Instead of a meaningless life that will be forgotten after it is over, Jesus's wisdom from above holds out the possibility of a life that matters more than we can imagine. In the words of C. S. Lewis, our lives and work are intended to be the beginning of something "which goes on forever: in which every chapter is better than the one before."

3

WISDOM AND HUMILITY

What do we mean when we say that someone is humble? Several years ago, I gave a talk on leadership to a class of students. Afterward, a student came up to me and said, "You seem like a humble person." I answered without thinking, "Well, I was until you told me!"

I've thought about that exchange over the years. What the student meant was that I was being modest. In my talk, I had primarily focused on others' successes and my failures. And I also thought about my instinctive response. At that moment, humility meant not thinking too much about myself. Being humble seemed to me an unself-conscious trait. In other words, you couldn't be humble if you are aware of how humble you are!

Is that all humility is—how we think about ourselves? Are modesty and humility the same thing?

THE WISDOM OF HUMILITY

In his book *Humilitas*, historian John Dickson argues that humility is more than modesty or self-deprecation. According to Dickson, humility is: "*The noble choice to forgo your status, deploy your resources or use your influence for the good of others before yourself*."[1]

In other words, humility acts for the benefit of others even when that costs us something. Humility is an action more than a feeling about how "humble" we are.

His definition also helpfully distinguishes between humility as a choice and humiliation as an experience of coercion. In a related insight, it implicitly acknowledges the worth of the one choosing to be humble. Jesus seminally illustrates Dickson's definition as he describes the Roman crucifixion that awaited him: "No one takes [my life] from me, but I lay it down of my own accord. I have power to lay it down, and I have power to take it up again" (John 10:18).

As Jesus himself suggests, humility is about the proper use of power. It is about how we use our status, our resources, and our influence for the sake of others. Humility is *not* about having low self-esteem as a leader or being a doormat. And it is undoubtedly not about imposing "humility" on others by coercion.

Power and humility are often viewed as mutually exclusive. One of the central theses of this book is that they need not be. *Wise leadership embodies real power with genuine humility.*

When I first stepped into management, I became friends with a fellow leader who happened to be a Christian. Pete was a more experienced manager, and I admired how he lived out his faith in the context of his leadership responsibilities. We often talked about the challenges of being organizational leaders. One day, he surprised me by saying, "You know, Uli, it's not hard being a leader if you don't mind being a son of a bitch!" His candor shocked me into silence. But what he said stuck with me. Pete captured the challenge of wielding power with humility in one memorable saying.

Even though we may feel bad about it, using power without humility seems necessary and inevitable to many of us. Others expect

---

1. John Dickson, *Humilitas: A Lost Key to Life, Love, and Leadership* (Grand Rapids: Zondervan, 2009), 24.

it of us, even though they too might prefer otherwise. As George C. Scott said as the lead character in the movie *Patton*: "I may be a son of a bitch, but at least I'm their son of a bitch!" Most people would agree. It seems that leadership sometimes requires power to be used without the consideration of humility.

In the ancient world, people valued modesty but not humility. And they loved honor above all. As Dickson points out, "Humility before an equal or a lesser was morally suspect. It upset the assumed equation: merit demanded honour, thus honour was the proof of merit. Avoiding honour implied a diminishment of merit. It was shameful. . . . [So] the Romans distinguished between *modestia* and *humilitas*. The former was a dignified restraint, the latter a shameful lowering."[2]

In other words, humility wasn't just foolish, it was wrong. It upset the moral framework of society. As Dickson observes, it took Jesus's example on the cross to change the minds of many. "The crucifixion was . . . proof that greatness can express itself in humility . . . the noble choice to lower yourself for the sake of others."[3]

Dickson argues that Jesus's life and death changed the trajectory of human history. Jesus made the use of power for others through self-sacrifice a viable alternative to the imposition of self-will through violence and coercion.[4] Those who follow Jesus are called to follow his example and not merely to look to Jesus's sacrifice as something for their advantage.

Humility, in that sense, is at the heart of a Christian vision of leadership. It is also at the heart of what it means to be a wise leader. The crucifixion not only embodies humility in the singular event for our benefit, but it singularly demonstrates a new way of leadership — with humility at its center.

2. Dickson, *Humilitas*, 89–90.
3. Dickson, *Humilitas*, 107.
4. For an artistic portrayal, see, for example, Matthias Grünewald, *The Crucifixion*, 1523–1524, available at https://depree.org/wise-leader/image-6.

Humility in the "Real World"

But can humility "work" in the real world? Is it merely an idealistic vision best left to our religious duties? Or can it make a difference in helping organizations flourish? How, for example, might humility play out in business?

In research published in the book *Good to Great*, Jim Collins and his team discovered an unexpected result. They found that senior executives who displayed "deep humility" along with "fierce resolve"—whom Collins coined "Level 5 Leaders"—were crucial for companies that consistently outperformed their competitors.

In the *Harvard Business Review* summary of their research, Collins observes two aspects of the conclusion that surprised them. First, the character of an executive leader can have a profound impact on the long-term financial performance of a company. And second, humility is central to the kind of leader that would make such a difference.[5]

While Collins's description of humility may not be identical to Dickson's, they are sufficiently similar to make my point. The leaders described in Collins's research were the most senior executives in their organizations. They had the freedom (and perhaps even the expectation) to not behave in a humble manner. Instead, for various reasons, they chose to be humble rather than arrogant. And their humility was not mere personal modesty (although it might be seen that way). It exhibited itself in action.

Their actions focused on the organization's well-being and the people they led rather than on themselves and their reputation. They provide helpful examples of how humility can lead to organizational flourishing, even in highly competitive businesses.

It's worth noting that none of the executives were naively humble. In each case, they were shrewd businesspeople. *Importantly, humility*

5. James C. Collins, "Level 5 Leadership: The Triumph of Humility and Fierce Resolve," *Harvard Business Review* 79, no. 1 (2005): 66.

and shrewdness are not incompatible. Jesus himself, consistent with the biblical wisdom tradition on that score, encouraged his followers not to be simpleminded: "I am sending you out like sheep among wolves. Therefore be as shrewd as snakes and as innocent as doves" (Matt. 10:16 NIV).

Wisdom requires both shrewdness and innocence, two words that don't usually go together. Humility must be exercised with mature discernment. The apostle Paul, likely aware of Jesus's teaching on this matter, says it this way: "Brothers and sisters, do not be children in your thinking; rather, be infants in evil, but in thinking be adults" (1 Cor. 14:20).

Paradoxically, for followers of Jesus, a childlike innocence about participation in evil must be accompanied by thoughtful and nuanced actions. In that sense, wise decision making isn't easy. Both good and evil are complicated, and we dare not be naive or simpleminded about either.

Given that Collins's research was focused on CEOs, a natural question might be whether humility makes a difference if one is not in a senior role. How might deep humility and fierce resolve work themselves out in the lower echelons of an organization?

Marena joined our company as a software tester. In many software organizations at the time, software testing was neither a prized nor a privileged role. Plus, she joined the organization without much experience. Nevertheless, she quickly distinguished herself in the role. She became legendary for wanting to get the last bug out of each software release. And her fierce resolve was matched by a genuine humility in her work.

In our company, we took great pride in delivering exceptionally reliable software. As a software tester in that culture, Marena could have used her role to browbeat software developers, but she didn't. Her surprising gentleness and relentless commitment to excellence won many over, whereas others in similar roles only raised developers' hackles. Her example and influence permeated our software quality team and shaped our company's reputation as a provider of high-reliability software for our customers. She is an excellent example of what deep humility and fierce resolve can do at any level of an organization.

But what if, despite our best efforts, humility just doesn't seem to work? What if humility doesn't lead to flourishing in our organizational context but only seems to make things worse? As I suggested earlier, these are complex questions that require careful discernment. We will explore these complexities more in chapter 6, on wisdom and leadership formation. For now, two fundamentally different approaches to our work are worth considering.

The first is illustrated in the fifth movie of the *Star Wars* anthology, *The Empire Strikes Back*. In the film, Jedi Master Yoda trains young Luke Skywalker to be a Jedi knight. At one point, Luke tries to raise his X-Wing fighter from the swamp by using the Force but fails. He complains that he tried his best but couldn't do it. Yoda responds, "Do or do not. There is no try."

In a nutshell, that summarizes one way of looking at our work. It's all about results, not about the effort. Either you succeed, or you don't. Trying hard doesn't matter.

In contrast, the poet T. S. Eliot captures an entirely different approach in his landmark work *The Four Quartets*: "There is only the trying. The rest is not our business."[6]

Eliot confronts us with an alternative vision in a culture that focuses almost exclusively on results. When humility doesn't seem to work, we are nevertheless called to live and work faithfully. Or, to say it a bit more accurately, when humility doesn't generate the results we expect, we should continue its practice because we believe that it's the right thing to do and that God can be trusted with the results.

During the recession that followed the financial crisis in 2008, our company was confronted with a painful reality. While we had had a long and mutually fruitful relationship with our principal

---

6. T. S. Eliot, "East Coker," in *The Complete Poems and Plays, 1909–1950* (New York: Harcourt Brace, 1980), 128.

customer, Herman Miller, the economic downturn put pressure on them to significantly reduce costs, including their investment in the technology we helped create for them. This was complicated by the fact that we had jointly developed a business model predicated on a proprietary rather than an open technology platform. In the words of an early observer of our relationship, we were joined at the hip. There were benefits and challenges for both organizations.

Starting in 2002, with Herman Miller's encouragement, we began to pursue creating an open platform. For many reasons, even though we made significant progress, it was a long journey. A Swedish competitor, Configura, had pursued an open technology platform from the beginning and had developed a growing following.

One option was to circle the wagons and simply leverage our relationship with Herman Miller as best we could. Indeed, the 2008 downturn stimulated creativity within our organization and our relationship with Herman Miller. But it eventually became clear that would not be enough, at least not enough for what our partner needed.

So, I began exploring alternative strategic opportunities with Configura and looking at ways to accelerate our company's open platform development. After much work and many conversations, we concluded that a strategic partnership with Configura wouldn't work. Our discussions, which included Herman Miller, led to their adoption of Configura as their new technology platform.

That's not the result I had hoped for. Still, we determined to remain a good business partner with Herman Miller and a charitable business competitor toward Configura. Our company did its best to finish well and facilitate Herman Miller's technology transition.

I hope that we did all that with individual and corporate humility. I'm pretty sure that we (or at least I) didn't feel particularly humble during some of that time. But, as best we could, we tried to act not only in our interest but also in the interest of our customer and even our competitor.

As I related earlier, I had a conversation with Max De Pree during that season. As Max wisely observed then, perhaps I needed to learn

to fail at something. And maybe a corollary to Max's insight is that
when we fail while being faithful, it may not be a failure after all.

Attitudes for Cultivating Humility

How do we practically cultivate humility in our leadership? Even
though humility is ultimately expressed in action, it begins by cultivating an appropriate attitude toward the world around us. Put
simply, we need to understand that (1) what we know has limits, and
(2) even what we think we know may be wrong. Some refer to this as
"epistemological humility."

First, *what we know has limits*. As noted in previous chapters, the
wisdom from above presumes that we acknowledge our finiteness
and limitations. Seeing clearly, one of the critical challenges of leadership, is always held in tension with the limits of our vision. As the
apostle Paul wrote, "Now we see in a mirror, dimly. . . . Now I know
only in part" (1 Cor. 13:12).

Those of us who claim to follow Jesus need to wrestle with the
limits of what we think we know. On the one hand, Jesus claims to
be the way, the truth, and the life. And this has universal implications
for everyone and everything. There is a long, rich written tradition
rooted in the teachings of Jesus himself, which claim to provide reliable wisdom for all human beings to follow.

But our faith, which should lead us to humility, can be distorted
into arrogance. We can come to believe that we are wise and everyone
who disagrees with us is foolish. Our faith can confuse relational
confidence in God with a propositional certainty about God. As
Dietrich Bonhoeffer wisely said, "Faith alone is certainty. Everything but faith is subject to doubt. Jesus Christ alone is the certainty
of faith."[7]

It is helpful to remember that faith is an expression of personal
trust in another person rather than simply giving intellectual assent

---

7. Quoted in Lesslie Newbigin, *Proper Confidence: Faith, Doubt, and Certainty in Christian Discipleship* (Grand Rapids: Eerdmans, 1995), i.

to a set of facts. That relationship requires vulnerability, risk, and, most of all, trust in another person. God is entirely free to be God and is not beholden to our expectations. While we can be confident in God's character, the wisdom from above reminds us to be appropriately humble in what we think we know.

For Bonhoeffer, a lifelong pacifist, that meant wrestling with how to respond faithfully to the Nazi regime. Instead of remaining safely at a distance when Union Theological Seminary invited him to stay in the United States in 1939, he opted to return to Germany and became involved in a resistance network while simultaneously working for the Nazi intelligence agency.

Ultimately, he was accused of participating in a plot to assassinate Hitler and hanged as a result. Bonhoeffer's life and death are vivid examples of the difficult ambiguities of discerning wisely in the midst of the world's realities. As he wrote during that time: "Christians in Germany will face the terrible alternative of either willing the defeat of their nation in order that Christian civilization may survive, or willing the victory of their nation and thereby destroying our civilization. I know which of these alternatives I must choose; but I cannot make that choice in security."[8]

Seeking to follow Jesus from within the context of our often complex and messy lives underscores our need for faith in God and a healthy skepticism about ourselves and what we know. In the end, humility is about placing our hope in God and not in ourselves.

Cultivating humility also acknowledges that *even what we think we know may be wrong*. As human beings, we have limits to our knowledge. But our limitation is further complicated by our brokenness, which compromises our ability to decide wisely.

Unfortunately, our commitment to Jesus and our desire to resist evil can sometimes blind us to our complicity. As someone told me long ago, we need to be careful not to commit "the sins of the saints" where we mask our guilt with righteous indignation.

8. Eberhard Bethge, *Dietrich Bonhoeffer: A Biography*, rev. and ed. Victoria J. Barnett (Minneapolis: Fortress, 2000), 655.

We need to remember that only God is incorruptibly good. Nothing created, in itself, is so good that it cannot be distorted or corrupted. That's a surprising and painful lesson that the whole biblical narrative bears out. And humanity in the present world, even when redeemed by Christ, bears the mark of our brokenness. As Christians, even as we pursue justice in the world, we do well to remember that we are part of the problem. As the Russian writer Aleksandr Solzhenitsyn said, "If only it were all so simple! If only there were evil people somewhere insidiously committing evil deeds, and it were necessary only to separate them from the rest of us and destroy them. But *the line dividing good and evil cuts through the heart of every human being.* And who is willing to destroy a piece of his own heart?"[9]

That insight should restrain our inclination as leaders to arrogance and hubris. For those of us who claim to follow Jesus, it should also motivate us to a regular practice of reflection and self-examination.

Practically, these two foundational attitudes require that we develop a community of truth-tellers in our leadership circle. In my experience, the more responsibilities I take on, the more reluctant people become to tell me the truth about myself. People become more cautious and less forthcoming regarding my blind spots.

After the recent merger of two large nonprofit health entities, I had the privilege of becoming the board chair of the combined system. One of the first things I did was have one-on-one conversations with each new board member. Some of them I knew previously; some I did not. But in each case, I explicitly acknowledged that I had my blind spots and invited them to provide feedback when they saw something that I did not. I know that's not a once-for-all conversation. I also know that much will depend on how I respond to people's constructive feedback when it comes. But I hope by setting that tone early in our relationship, others will be more open with me than they might otherwise.

9. Aleksandr Solzhenitsyn, *The Gulag Archipelago, 1918–1956: An Experiment in Literary Investigation* (New York: Harper Perennial Modern Classics, 2007), 168 (emphasis added).

Practices That Cultivate Humility

In addition to the above attitudes, I've found five leadership practices helpful in developing humility. Many of them deal with leadership situations with significant differences or conflicts. They do not come easy to me, as I suspect they will not for most leaders. Humility takes intentionality and effort on our part.

1.   Exhibit genuine curiosity about others and their differences.

Because humility is rooted in concern for the other, cultivating humility begins with trying to understand those who are different from us. I naturally gravitate toward those who are like me. But in leadership, we are called to lead a team of people, many of whom differ from us, sometimes in profound ways.

A sign of healthy leadership is the ability to nurture a diverse group in perspectives and gifts. That isn't easy to do without a healthy curiosity about those different from us and a willingness to appreciate what those differences contribute to the team.

I started a company with a good friend. He and I had known each other for many years. We shared many interests, including a passion for forming an entrepreneurial venture. In many ways, I thought we were alike.

But once we went into business together, I discovered we were pretty different in how we approached our business relationships. I valued consensus and agreement. He, on the other hand, loved to be a contrarian. He took the opposite position on almost anything that mattered, whatever my view was. Mind you, he did it in a friendly way. But he rarely let my discomfort stand in the way of a good argument. I have to admit that sometimes I found it tiring, if not downright frustrating.

But I quickly learned that this was not just a matter of him wanting to be right. Or that he simply enjoyed a good debate. Instead, he wanted to make sure we had critically thought through essential issues. Because he didn't let me off the hook, his contrarian approach made sure we worked through the critical aspects of significant decisions. I came to appreciate, however uncomfortably, that our business benefited from a perspective and practice that was contrary to my own.

That experience has helped me create space for those different from me. And I don't mean just being tolerant of others who are different but learning to be actively curious about why others are different and how that difference might contribute to the common good.

It didn't take much for me to understand why my business partner did what he did and how that helped our business succeed. But at other times, that may not be so clear. That's why curiosity is essential. It often takes time and considerable effort to understand and appreciate those different from us. And in the process of doing so, we cultivate humility.

A complementary aspect of being curious about others is being honest about ourselves. As we discover what makes others different from us, and why that might be a good thing, we find aspects of ourselves that may be less than flattering.

I discovered that my self-perceived "virtue" of consensus building sometimes hid an unhealthy aversion to dealing with thorny issues. Sometimes I was going along to get along. What I initially saw in my business partner as resistance to consensus building, I came to appreciate as a challenge for me to do the right thing. My virtue turned out not to be so virtuous after all. Or, to quote T. S. Eliot, I discovered

> Things ill done and done to others' harm
> Which once you took for exercise of virtue.
> Then fools' approval stings, and honour stains.[10]

---

10. T. S. Eliot, "Little Gidding," in *Complete Poems and Plays*, 142.

2. *When there is disagreement, let each person define their views.*

It's easy to assume that we already know someone else's perspective going into a conversation. We just "know" what they think. Of course, not only is that presumptuous, but it often leads to arguing with someone other than the person in front of us. Paying careful attention to what someone believes is a lot harder.

One practice that I've found helpful is an extension of the practice of active listening. In that discipline, we try to repeat to people what they've said to us. That's relatively easy with simple things, like what someone had for dinner last night. But it's more complex when dealing with people's values and beliefs. It requires work to get into their heads to understand what they are saying. So, in addition to allowing people to define their views rather than projecting what we think they are, it's helpful to try and restate in our own words what we understand of their convictions and ask, "Is this what you mean? Do I have this right?"

Frankly, I find it much easier to engage in critique rather than in trying to understand what others believe. I have my arguments all lined up for an imagined interlocutor, often before I even enter the conversation. It's hard work to understand another's point of view when it is so different from mine, especially when it represents a deep conflict in values or belief systems. But that too is the price for learning humility.

A related practice is to compare our best arguments with their best arguments, rather than our best with their worst. When we are in a leadership situation where there are different sides to a conflict, all sides usually have good and not-so-good arguments. Sometimes the disputes can be settled on their merits. But often, particularly in a polarized or distrustful context, we need to find some way to bridge the lack of trust.

A helpful starting point is to focus on the strong points of each argument instead of on its weaknesses. Taking the point of view of others seriously means acknowledging the strength of their ideas, even when they counter our perceived interests. Humility means subordinating our interests long enough to hear what others are saying, and in a way that we might not have considered before.

    3.   Build trust and agree when possible.

    Forming and growing trust are at the heart of leadership. Without trust, authentic leadership is impossible. When there is disagreement, figuring out a way to create a safe space for difficult conversations is one of the tasks of wise leadership. Sometimes it can lead to surprising situations and results.

    Richard Mouw was the president of Fuller Seminary and is a good friend. He is an exceptionally articulate statesman and passionate advocate for historic Christianity who—to the surprise of many and the dismay of some—opened a serious dialogue with the Mormon church some years ago.

    As I heard Rich tell the story, he had developed a relationship with some senior leaders in the Mormon theological community at Brigham Young University (BYU). As part of building that relationship, they decided to host an event at BYU between Rich and some of his PhD students, representing Fuller, and their counterparts from Brigham Young.

    One day, they gathered for a chapel event. One of the New Testament professors from BYU preached a sermon out of Paul's letter to the Galatians. Rich commented afterward that he found the sermon surprisingly orthodox in content and one that any Christian pastor could have preached. One of his students reportedly turned to one of the Brigham Young students and said, "I didn't know that Mormons believed this about the Bible." And the BYU student responded, "I didn't either!"[11]

    When we create a safe space and trusted relationships, everyone can sometimes be surprised by what we learn about others, not to

---

11. Thanks to Richard Mouw for sharing this in a personal conversation.

mention ourselves! Of course, Rich would be the first to say that serious theological differences between orthodox Christian and Mormon beliefs remain. And yet, there are places, some of them surprising to both sides, where agreement is possible. But it took humility, along with the associated risks, to find them.

4.   *Own your own responsibility.*

Given humility's focus on the other person, it may be surprising to have a practice that zeros in on us. Taking personal responsibility is work that cannot be delegated to others—it is ours alone to bear.

When Rich was president of Fuller Seminary, Bill Robinson was president of Whitworth University. Bill became a good friend while we served together on Fuller Seminary's De Pree Leadership Center Board.

Bill tells the story of Whitworth wrestling with the question of whether the university would put filters on the Internet. Campus-wide conversations about the issue took place over much of the 1995/1996 academic year, culminating in a town hall meeting. At that time, a student asked whether they were now going to have a chance to vote on what the university's policy should be. Because of how participative the conversations had been, Bill's response caught the student by surprise. Bill said that while he wanted to get every-one's input, he was responsible for doing what he believed was in the institution's best interest. And that was a responsibility he carried as president and couldn't delegate to a vote by the students. For better or for worse, Bill owned that responsibility.[12]

Humility is not the abdication of personal responsibility. Com-munal participation in discernment doesn't preclude decision-making responsibility from being vested in one person. We can't use the former as a shield against making the hard decisions we alone must make. Humility doesn't arrogantly take on too much responsi-bility, nor does it skirt that which is ours to carry.

12. Thanks to Bill Robinson for sharing this in a personal conversation.

Earlier, I discussed the problematic season at my company pre-
cipitated by the recession of 2008. During that time, I convened our
senior leaders to discuss how we might address the technology and
business challenges we faced. We had a long conversation, with many
different options and opinions presented, some with great passion.
Somewhere along the line, I wondered whether I would be able to
get the leadership team to unite behind a single course of action
going forward.

In the end, I thanked them for their input and said, "Now, here
is what we are going to do . . ." A bit to my surprise, there was little
resistance or second-guessing. Taking responsibility is essential, not
least because it provides focus and clarity.

    5.   *Exhibit vulnerability.*

> Do not let me hear
>   Of the wisdom of old men, but rather of their folly,
>   Their fear of fear and frenzy, their fear of possession,
>   Of belonging to another, or to others, or to God.[13]

I like talking about my successes. While active in my software
business, I enjoyed talking about the latest features we had developed, the growth of our customer base, and our ability to attract the
best and brightest technologists.

In my work in health-care governance, I like to talk about how
we are taking care of the most vulnerable in our communities, how
our doctors and nurses saved lives during the COVID pandemic,
and how we are making health care better and more affordable.

In my faith community, I like to focus on the new young families
who are joining our church, the great new pastor we just hired, and
the effectiveness of our programs in dealing with the physical and
spiritual needs of our wider community.

13. Eliot, "East Coker," 125–26.

But I don't like talking about failures. And I notice others don't either.

As leaders, we are especially reluctant to talk about the interior dimension of our failures. We are afraid of how our uncertainties and fears may affect others. We fear that we will infect those we are called to lead with fear and anxiety that cause them to panic. In Eliot's words, we have a "fear of fear and frenzy."

All that is understandable. We neither want to create unnecessary fear in others nor do we want to burden others with the burden that is ours to carry as leaders. Nevertheless, if we focus only on the positive, our leadership loses something important.[14]

At the height of our partnership with Herman Miller in 2002, I got a call from their CEO. I flew out to meet with him and some of his senior executives to discuss their level of investment in the technology we had developed. In the shadow of both the dot-com bubble bursting in 1999 and the events of 9/11, Herman Miller was reevaluating all their spending, including their work with us, even though it was an essential part of their business strategy. It became clear that we had to make a significant adjustment in our staffing to accommodate their investment reduction.

On the flight home from Grand Rapids to Seattle, I wrestled with what I would tell my staff. At that time, I didn't know the exact size of the reduction or the particular people who would be affected. One approach was to say nothing until things became clearer. After all, why raise the anxiety of everyone over something uncertain and over which they had no control? Why make the vital work they were doing more difficult and thereby risk making matters worse? But I chose a different approach.

After returning to Seattle, I assembled the team and told them what I knew and what I didn't know. I told them that a significant cut was coming, likely affecting up to a third of our team. I told them

14. James C. Collinson, "Prozac Leadership and the Limits of Positive Thinking," *Sage Journals: Leadership* 8, no. 2 (2012): 87–107.

I would keep them informed on the details as they became available. I also told them that, given the reduction size, I didn't feel right withholding that information even though uncertainties were involved. I asked them to continue focusing on their essential work so that we wouldn't make things worse for everyone. I also asked anyone who was thinking about changing jobs to let me know so that we could factor that into our staffing plan.

It felt like the right thing to do, but I knew it was risky. I thought they could handle the uncertainty. But even I was surprised by people's responses. Several offered to adjust their hours so we could keep more staff. One person said he had been considering a move and wanted to let me know so someone else could stay.

But perhaps one of the most extraordinary responses came from Marena, the software tester I wrote about earlier. After the staff meeting, she asked to see me privately. I thought that, as one of the more junior people at the time, she was concerned about her job and wanted to know how safe she was in light of the future reductions. Instead, she said, "I know how hard it must have been for you to share that news with us. I just wanted to see if you are ok."

At first, I wasn't sure I had heard her right. Her job was at risk, and she was concerned about my welfare? I was deeply moved by her remarkable demonstration of concern for the well-being of another, even in the face of her own loss. Ever since, her humility has challenged me to go and do likewise.

I recognize that the above story is about changing external business circumstances and doesn't address how humility should help us deal with our moral failures as leaders. It's surprising how difficult it is for Christian leaders to be candid about their moral failures.

You'd think we who believe that our sins have been forgiven for eternity would find it easier to admit them in time. But time and again, that proves not to be so. Like our archetypal ancestors, when faced with the consequences of our moral failures, our instinct is to hide ourselves and blame others. Yet it need not be so.

Two redemptive examples from our faith traditions are helpful. I find it very encouraging that the canonical gospel writers didn't edit out Peter's threefold denial to protect one of the pillars of the early church. Since the tradition that formed the Gospels likely included stories from Peter himself, I suspect those close to him made sure the stories didn't get cleaned up to improve his image. If anything, Peter's "fear and folly" have been preserved as a reminder that none of us need shrink from our failures. After all, Jesus's threefold restoration matched Peter's threefold denials (John 21:15–19). Jesus's grace more than matches our most profound failures when they are faced honestly and openly.

Another comes from one of my favorite novels by Frederick Buechner. *Godric* is a story about the twelfth-century saint. Buechner imaginatively adopts the point of view of a church biographer recording the story of Godric's life. One of the story's key themes is the contrast between the official church biography and the story Godric tells of what actually happened.

As Buechner's novel illustrates, it's easy to whitewash our leadership story and thereby deprive us of its power. Godric's real story is not only more believable, but it's more helpful and transformative for others. That's a valuable lesson for those of us in leadership who struggle with being genuinely vulnerable to others. As Eliot says in his poem:

> The only wisdom we can hope to acquire
> Is the wisdom of humility: humility is endless.[15]

HUMILITY AS THE PRIMARY VIRTUE OF LEADERSHIP

Saint Augustine wrote that the three essential ways to pursue truth and wisdom are: "first humility, second humility, third humility."[16] Based on my struggles with this most difficult leadership virtue, I couldn't agree more. In our North American leadership culture

---

15. Eliot, "East Coker," 126.
16. Quote from *Letters (83–130)*, ed. Roy Joseph Deferrari, trans. Wilfrid Parsons, The Fathers of the Church, vol. 18 (Washington, DC: Catholic University of America Press, 1953), 282, https://theoldguys.org/2019/07/05/augustine-humility-humility-humility.

that often values hubris over humility, humility becomes more important even as it becomes more difficult.

Perhaps now more than ever before, those of us who claim to
follow Jesus need to recover humility at the center of our leadership
practice. There's no question that it is difficult. It has always been
difficult. And it was no more difficult than when confronted with
the example of Jesus himself.

I love Ford Madox Brown's painting *Jesus Washing Peter's Feet*.[17]
In Jesus's day, as John Dickson noted earlier, for a rabbi like Jesus to
wash his followers' feet—a task usually reserved for the lowest of
household servants—was shameful. This painting wonderfully captures the astonishment and dismay of Jesus's disciples as Jesus washed
Peter's feet. If you look at the painting, you will notice their shocked
reaction as they watch Jesus in action. I particularly love the look on
Peter's face. He looks as if to say, "This feels *so* wrong."

Of course, it was wrong at that moment in history, even for his
closest followers. Jesus announced and practiced a radically different
vision of leadership. It was not mere simile, much less hyperbole,
when Jesus said: "The greatest among you must become like the
youngest, and the leader like one who serves" (Luke 22:26).

But despite how difficult it was to follow, humility quickly became the distinguishing characteristic of life in the early church. So
much so that both Peter and James, two people who were closest
to Jesus, learned and taught this fundamental leadership virtue. In
precisely the same words in two different apostolic letters to the early
church, Peter and James say,

> "God opposes the proud,
>   but gives grace to the humble." (1 Pet. 5:5; James 4:6)

---

17. Ford Madox Brown, *Jesus Washing Peter's Feet*, 1852–1856, available at
https://depree.org/wise-leader/image-7.

4

Wisdom and Different Kinds of Power

When the third and final installment of Peter Jackson's movie trilogy *The Lord of the Rings* came out, everyone in my software company was filled with anticipation. We closed the office for a day to see the newly released movie at Seattle's iconic Cinerama theater. *The Return of the King* did not disappoint. And that day still lives in my memory almost two decades later.

Jackson's movie trilogy raised J. R. R. Tolkien's literary work to the status of a modern mythic tale. Its rich and imaginative story embodies the ancient conflict between good and evil, as it tells of the use and abuse of power. As Tolkien wrote, "You can make the Ring into an allegory of our own time, if you like: an allegory of the inevitable fate that waits for all attempts to defeat evil power by power."[1]

Having lived through the barbarism of the two world wars of the early twentieth century, Tolkien understandably saw "power [as] an ominous and sinister word in all these tales."[2] Tolkien would likely have agreed with Lord Acton's famous maxim that "power tends to corrupt, and absolute power corrupts absolutely."[3]

1. *The Letters of J. R. R. Tolkien*, ed. Humphrey Carpenter (New York: Houghton Mifflin, 2000), 121.
2. *The Letters of J. R. R. Tolkien*, 152.
3. Quoted in "John Dalberg-Acton, 1st Baron Acton," Wikipedia, last edited June 12, 2023, https://en.wikipedia.org/wiki/John_Dalberg-Acton,_1st _Baron_Acton#cite_note-lmcone-4.

Like Tolkien, many today view power with deep misgivings. Often, power is used in destructive ways. While the results of abusive power are undeniable, need power always be seen as intrinsically suspicious or even evil? I think there are reasons to believe otherwise.

To begin with, if power is defined as the *capacity to affect something else*, then power is intrinsic to God's good creation. For example, all matter and energy in the universe possess gravity's effect or "power." Gravity is what allows the universe to take its particular shape. And it is critical to the ongoing life on our planet. Without it, the universe would neither have developed nor been sustainable. At the level of the inanimate creation, God's creation of the power of gravity is an observable good for which we can be grateful.

The same is true for the animate creation. Life exists in complex relationships that we call "ecosystems." Ecosystems represent biological relationships between various living organisms and their inanimate habitats. Foundational to the notion of an ecosystem is that these living organisms and the elements of their habitat each exert an influence on the other. That effect or power contributes to the functioning of the ecology of the whole. The rich and diverse ecosystems found on our planet are a testament to the goodness of the natural order that God's creative power makes possible.

But what about power exercised by moral agents, such as human beings? Hasn't our recurring history of violence demonstrated that human power should always be viewed with suspicion? And for those who take Jesus's teaching seriously, didn't Jesus come to demonstrate a way of humility that is the antithesis of the exercise of power?

As the first question suggests, the exercise of power by moral agents presumes the capacity to do evil as well as to do good. Consequently, power need not be exercised for good, despite the Creator's intentions. And the biblical witness suggests that humanity has not just made some bad choices along the way but, in that process, has corrupted its capacity to use its power well. In that sense, our experience of power is much as Tolkien described it: "an ominous and sinister word."

But, contrary to the conceptions of some, Jesus does not reject the exercise of power. Instead, Jesus recovers a vision for its humane usage. And although humility is essential to Jesus's teachings, he also uses power in spectacular ways. Jesus raises people from the dead, heals them from dreadful diseases, and delivers them from oppressive spiritual forces. The Gospels are full of stories that demonstrate Jesus's extraordinary combination of both power and humility.

Such acts of power are regularly and rightly seen as witnesses to Jesus's divinity. But rarely are those same acts seen as an expression of Jesus's humanity, or perhaps even more helpfully, as God's intention to empower all human beings. But that is the thrust of the biblical story. From the very beginning, God's explicit intention involves human beings exercising power on God's behalf for the sake of the world. In the original creation account, God charges human beings, male and female: "Be fruitful and multiply, and fill the earth and *subdue* it; and have *dominion* over the fish of the sea and over the birds of the air and over every living thing that moves upon the earth" (Gen. 1:28).

While "subdue" and "dominion" could imply oppressive control and domination, the rest of the biblical account underscores the importance of that power being exercised for the benefit of others. God's creation mandate requires humans to exercise power. And that mandate continues to the very end of the biblical story. The very last words said about the vocation of human beings are these: "And they will reign forever and ever" (Rev. 22:5).

From beginning to end, leadership and the exercise of power, in their infinite varieties, are essential to a biblical vision of being human.

So, the critical question is this: What does the wise exercise of power look like?

A HEALTHY VISION OF POWER

As the above introduction suggests, a healthy vision of power stands in contrast to two different and opposite postures toward power.

Tolkien's *The Lord of the Rings* provides helpful imagery to illustrate them both.

First, a healthy view of power opposes an obsession with power. In Tolkien's story, those who take up the Ring of Power inevitably say to the ring: "My Precious!" And that obsession with power turns out to be a form of enslavement. Obsession turns power's promise of freedom into a dark dominion over the one who "possesses" it. The inscription of Tolkien's Ring of Power memorably describes the result: "One ring to rule them all . . . and in the darkness bind them."

Second, a healthy vision of power also opposes a blanket rejection of power. In Tolkien's epic tale, destroying the Ring of Power is not the same as eliminating all power. Even after the destruction of the One Ring, human beings in Middle Earth still had rulers who had to exercise power well.

More interesting still, the need to destroy the Ring of Power provides suggestive imagery on dealing with power's toxic effects. Not just anyone can handle the ring. Only Frodo, a humble hobbit, can carry the ring to its destruction. And even he is affected by it. As the character of Frodo suggests, *while humility is essential* to mitigating power's pernicious effects, humility alone is not enough. In the end, *power itself must be transformed* by the destruction of the ring and its old desire to dominate others, thereby leaving a different kind of power in the world that desires to serve the flourishing of others.

Perhaps most interesting, Frodo's journey to destroy the Ring of Power provides another insight. Like Frodo, we all carry power imperfectly and despite our weaknesses. At several points in the trilogy, Frodo tries to rid himself of the burden of the ring. Each time others remind him that he alone is the ring bearer. That's suggestive of an important insight.

Even though power can be corrosive and potentially corrupting, we are not thereby released from the obligation to carry it. Simply abdicating our responsibility is not the answer. In our weakness and humility, as modeled by Frodo, *power must be carried imperfectly even as we seek its radical transformation.* Perhaps that's another way of understanding God's encouragement to Paul, "My grace is sufficient for you, for my power is made perfect in weakness" (2 Cor. 12:9).

So, what does such transformed power look like in practice? Or, to ask the question in a slightly different way, what are models for the right use of power?

In exploring that question, I am indebted to Andy Crouch's book *Playing God: Redeeming the Gift of Power*. It started me on a journey of thinking about healthy conceptions of power that led to some of the reflections in this chapter and the next.

In his musings on the creation account,[4] Crouch describes two different models of power based on phrases found in Genesis 1: "Let there be" (Gen. 1:3, 6, 14) and "Let us make" (Gen. 1:26). I describe these below as the "generative" and "participative" models of power. These two, along with the more traditional "directive" model, will frame my reflections on how healthy power can be exercised in practice.

GENERATIVE POWER

One of the most astonishing insights of the Genesis creation account is that God chose to create. As theologians have long commented, God didn't create out of a sense of necessity. In other words, God wasn't lonely or bored. God chose to create freely and willingly. And, perhaps even more surprisingly, God has a deep personal affection for, and connection with, all that has been created. As noted earlier, God's "compassion is over all that he has made" (Ps. 145:9).

In the biblical narrative, God grants to the universe a state of being that is separate and distinct from God, but in a way that the universe embodies many attributes that reflect his nature. The universe is vast and beautiful. It is mysterious but deeply ordered and dependable. It is not utterly chaotic and capricious, which is one of the reasons that science has been possible and has left such a profound imprint on modern culture.

---

4. Andy Crouch, *Playing God: Redeeming the Gift of Power* (Downers Grove, IL: InterVarsity Press, 2013), 32–35.

From a human point of view, there is no reason that the universe should have turned out that way. And for much of human history, the notion that the universe was reliable enough as an independent object of study distinct from the potentially capricious actions of a pantheon of gods would have seemed implausible. Perhaps even ludicrous. Arguably, the biblical revelation of a reliable God who created a reliable physical universe provided the intellectual framework for the rise of modern science.

In addition to creating an inanimate universe distinct from God's own being, the biblical narrative also describes the creation of a similar but animate universe. Living creatures of all kinds were created with the inherent generativity to sustain their own kind. Rather than God directly creating each new creature, remarkably, God grants each living creature the capacity to reproduce. From the very beginning, *life is given generative power*. In every living creature's capacity for a generative act, there is an echo of God's primal "Let there be . . ."

Finally, in what seems to be the ultimate demonstration of generative power, God creates living creatures with moral agency. Unimaginably, God creates human beings who can say no as well as yes to God.

God's own innate freedom to choose whom and what to desire and love is given to one of God's creatures. And implicit in that generative act is the risk of choosing—in the middle of a very good creation—what is "not good." It is an astonishingly risky act of faith on God's part and provides the heart and heartache of the drama that the scriptural narrative unfolds.

So, the created universe—inanimate, animate, and moral creatures—all incorporate and in various ways exhibit the generative power that God exercises in the creation itself. And what is distinctive and essential to our understanding of generative power is that it is multiplicative. Unlike many conceptions of power, ancient and modern, generative power is not a zero-sum game.

Instead, *healthy power is inherently generous*, focused on sharing its creative power with others rather than hoarding power for itself. I believe generative power is the most fundamental of the biblical models of power, as evidenced in its repeated occurrence in the creation narrative itself. Indeed, "Let there be" is the first and most well-known literary refrain of Genesis 1. Practically, that means wisdom looks for ways to increase and broaden others' participation in power rather than trying to contain or restrict their scope.

Let me provide a small illustration from my work in board governance. One of the most significant challenges in corporate governance has been diversifying the composition of and participation on corporate boards. Historically, many corporate boards have struggled to move meaningfully beyond a White male demographic. Identifying and attracting potential board members who are different from ourselves is not easy. Forming a working community of leaders who take differing perspectives and voices seriously is even harder.

Many board members I know, myself included, have grown up with and adopted an assertive, extroverted leadership style. Others who have much to contribute come from more deferential, reflective leadership cultures. Consequently, it is easy for the latter voices to be effectively muted even when they are at the table.

To counter that effect in my work as board chair, I've cultivated a practice where everyone has time and space to offer substantive feedback and questions at the end of each board meeting. Further, when there are significant issues under discussion, I intentionally invite those who are less outspoken to offer their perspectives. These are very small steps to model generative power. But they are effective and easy to implement. And I have found them appreciated by all my board colleagues, whatever their leadership style.

No doubt, there are an infinite variety of ways to practice the exercise of generative power. Part of our creative challenge as leaders is to discover and employ them.

One other aspect of generative power is worth noting. As Crouch observes, "The Creator is not seeking a world full of pets. . . . He delights in wildness."[5] What might God's "delight in wildness" tell us about being wise leaders? I would suggest two related possibilities.

5. Crouch, *Playing God*, 33.

First, human beings are called to explore and make sense of the world around us. While not entirely incomprehensible, it is mysterious and complex, pulsing with life that possesses a dynamism of its own. As a result, and as I noted in the previous chapter on humility, one of the critical faculties of wise leadership is *curiosity*. Learning to love and pay careful attention to God's creation is an ancient aspect of wisdom. Notably, the legendary knowledge attributed to ancient Israel's King Solomon included studying the animate creation: "He would speak of trees, from the cedar that is in the Lebanon to the hyssop that grows in the wall; he would speak of animals, and birds, and reptiles, and fish. People came from all the nations to hear the wisdom of Solomon; they came from all the kings of the earth who had heard of his wisdom" (1 Kings 4:33–34).

The echoes of the creation narrative—plants, animals, birds, reptiles, and fish—are unmistakable and a reminder that humanity's dominion is rooted in a curiosity that pays careful attention to the world that God has made. It is also worth noting that Solomon exhibits a practical (and not just a philosophical) curiosity that seems to anticipate the development of modern science millennia later.

Second, in the language of the creation narrative, we are called as human beings to shape and cultivate a garden out of a wilderness. As a Jewish friend once told me, "God gives us the raw materials with which to make something."

That's a helpful way of looking at the creation God calls "very good." Evidently, "very good" doesn't mean "finished." There is an intentional rawness and wildness to the good world that God creates. All that indicates that another critical faculty of wise leadership is *creativity*.

We are called to make something of the good world God has entrusted to our care. In the second part of the creation narrative in Genesis 2, the creation of humanity is described where "there was no one to till the ground" (Gen. 2:5). Consequently, "The LORD God took the man and put him in the garden of Eden to till it and keep it" (Gen. 2:15).

Human agency and stewardship figured in God's design for the created order. But humanity's calling involves more than simply maintaining an agrarian creation. Instead, the long story that begins with a garden in the first book of Genesis ends with a city in the final book of Revelation. And that story tells us of an expansive vision of humanity's role.

Humanity has the privilege and opportunity to participate in God's creative project that culminates in a vibrant city into which "the kings of the earth will bring their glory" and where "people will bring . . . the glory and the honor of the nations" (Rev. 21:24, 26). Biblical wisdom doesn't require a return to a simpler, more idyllic time. Instead, it engages the full range of human capacities to create a previously unimagined future.

In summary, God's generative power results in a creation with different kinds of power embodied within it: from the inanimate creation, such as physical matter and energy, which carries forces to influence other parts of the creation, to living creatures who embody God's generativity in their procreative capacity, to moral agents who can choose whom and what to love and desire.

All that suggests the wise use of power requires the willingness to create power for others to exercise. Rather than treating others like our servants, we serve others by allowing them to come into their own. At a very practical level, that means we must be willing to delegate power as well as responsibility to others. And in the end, we must be willing to bear the risk of failure on others' part.

IN THE NAME OF CHI-LLC

There's something about having your name on a company that changes things. In my case, the company's name is CHI-LLC. You probably know the saying, "It's not personal; it's business." When it's your name on the door, it *is* personal.

My reputation is at stake every day because of what people who work there do or don't do. For better or worse, their attitudes and behaviors affect

how the rest of the world sees me. In that sense, owning a company is a profound act of faith in your people. As Max De Pree said about leadership more
generally, we "abandon ourselves to the gifts that other people bring."*

This helps me understand what Jesus means when he tells us that we have
the power to act in his name. What matters most to me as a business owner is
that the people who work with me understand what we are trying to do (our
mission) and who we intend to be (our character). In their work, I need them
to embody the mission and character of our company.

That isn't an easy thing. There are myriads of complex decisions and issues
that need resolution daily. That's why it's important for those who work at my
company to know who I am and to understand my vision for the company
and the values that energize and constrain our shared work.

While I enter into some decisions personally, as you can imagine, most
of them are made by others. It is essential for them (and incidentally for me)
that they internalize the mission and character of the company in a way that
empowers them to make the decisions for themselves. In the end, they need
to learn what it means to act faithfully "in the name of CHI-LLC."

I give them the power to act in my name, and I share the risk of failure
when they do that poorly.

And Jesus does the same.

* Max De Pree, *Leadership Jazz* (New York: Doubleday, 2008), 125.

Participative Power

If we are not careful, we can see generative power as something impersonal. Perhaps, as in a Deist conception, God creates other beings
and then leaves them to do things entirely on their own. But then
we come to the culmination of the creation account and the words
"Let us make. . . ." Those words describe God's creative power, at its
height, exercised in a personal, participative way.

With all that we have learned about the size of the universe, our
modern secular conception sees humanity's place in the universe as

unremarkable, if not entirely insignificant. Human beings are merely one species, on one planet, in a minor solar system, in an unexceptional galaxy, set in a vast universe beyond imaginings. Perhaps the psalmist's question is more apt than ever before in human history:

> What are human beings that you are mindful of them,
> mortals that you care for them? (Ps. 8:4)

And yet, God does care. Seemingly out of proportion to humanity's place in the cosmos, God takes a particular interest in human beings. God creates humankind in a way unlike any other creature that we know of.

In the second creation account, God personally shapes humanity from the dirt of the ground (Gen. 2:7). In imagery repeated later in the biblical narrative, God describes humanity's creation as that of a sculptor creating a work of art out of earthen clay. It is a profoundly intimate portrait. God sculpts human beings out of the ground and breathes God's own life and spirit into them. In other words, God's hands get dirty. Creation doesn't get much more personal than that.

Or does it?

Previously, I noted that "compassionate" is God's first self-description. Hebrew scholars tell us that the word used there is related to a mother's womb.[6] As hard as it may be for us to fathom, God has feelings for us, much like a woman does for a child she has birthed. There is no more profound, more intimate metaphor in human experience available to describe God's creation and care for human beings.

In other words, a mother's compassion for her child beats at the heart of the universe. As the prophet Isaiah would later say in even stronger and more explicit terms:

6. John Goldingay, *Exodus & Leviticus for Everyone* (Louisville: Westminster John Knox, 2010), 124.

Can a woman forget her nursing child,
   or show no *compassion* for the child of her womb?
Even these may forget,
   yet I will not forget you. (Isa. 49:15)

That's an extraordinary self-disclosure on God's part. Like a mother, God deeply loves and has compassion for us. Despite how we might feel at any moment, the universe is not a cold, heartless place. God is not a Creator who could not care less: God is a Creator who could not care more.

So, what might all that suggest to us about how the gift of participative power should be exercised?

First, participative power is always *an expression of love*. Power is meant to be expressed personally, never impersonally. This may sound like countercultural wisdom, particularly in a business context where being personal sounds suspiciously like being emotionally enmeshed in our work or with our people. As I said earlier, the modern aphorism "It's not personal, it's just business" can provide a blanket cover for acting inhumanely.

To be clear, the love God has for us is the opposite of soft sentimentalism. Tough love is not a modern concept. It doesn't take much reading in the biblical material to see that God can be remarkably tough—even harsh—with people and in their circumstances.

But it is equally clear—particularly looked at through the lens of Jesus's life and death—that God's compassion is both behind and beneath God's tough love actions. As someone has aptly said, God's work in the world is sometimes a "severe mercy."

That should help us see how we might exercise power in the context of our leadership. Rather than cutting ourselves off emotionally from those we lead, we need to enter into those relationships with love and care, *and* act for the common good even when that's difficult.

One aspect of that difficulty is that our love and care have limits, given that we are finite creatures. And that means we have to discern what burdens we are to carry, what burdens we are to carry for others, and what burdens they must carry themselves. Paradoxically, in the words of T. S. Eliot, we must learn "to care and not to care."[7]

But the "and" is essential. We cannot merely "not care." Nor can we "care" all the time and for everyone. That, too, is part of learning the biblical wisdom of exercising power in love.

It helps me to think about this from my relationship as a father with my adult children and grandchildren. Even though I love them deeply, there inevitably come situations and circumstances where they need to experience the pain and suffering that are the consequence of their own actions. I don't intervene, not because I don't care, but because I want them to learn from their mistakes. And so they may not make even worse ones.

Even more difficult, at least for me, I sometimes need to deliberately expose them to difficulties or challenges that seem unfair to them at the moment, not because they've done something wrong but to help them develop and mature as human beings. No wonder parenting adult children and grandchildren is a prime training ground for learning the wise and loving use of participative power.

Second, participative power is *rooted in the community*. One of the most unhelpful and damaging images of power, both ancient and modern, is that it resides fundamentally in the individual. In such a vision, power becomes, at best, the work of heroic individuals working together occasionally for the common good.

In contemporary superhero mythology, the Avengers come to mind. Captain America is still Captain America, whether he is working together with the rest of the Avengers or not. So is Captain Marvel, Iron Man, or Black Widow. Even though there is a sense of community among them (at least some of the time!), their identities are not fundamentally shaped by their association with the Avengers.[8]

7. T. S. Eliot, "Ash Wednesday," in *The Complete Poems and Plays, 1909–1950* (New York: Harcourt Brace, 1980), 67.
8. My friend Mark Roberts (formerly executive director of the De Pree

But what if power is fundamentally vested in the community rather than brought in from the outside?

The apostle Paul uses the image of the human body as the foundational metaphor for how the human community is meant to operate. Yes, individuals have particular roles or gifts, but those gifts are rooted in the body's functioning. For example, the human heart has a specific function, but that role is only meaningful within the context of the body as a whole. No heart has a useful role outside the body. And so on for the eyes, the ears, the lungs, the liver, etc.

Such a perspective reminds us of the inherently relational and communal nature of power and leadership. As Max De Pree used to say, you can't be a leader if there are no followers. Not least in that sense, a leader is "a debtor."[9] That's helpful for seeing power—in this case, the power of leaders—in the context of a community rather than separate from it.

Even our capacity to exercise power is derived from the community. For example, a heart cannot function without blood vessels to provide it with nutrients and oxygen. A participative perspective of power recognizes that everyone is a debtor to the larger community of which they are a part.

That is especially challenging for those of us in more public roles. We easily delude ourselves into thinking we are heroic figures doing great work sustained by our own virtues and abilities. Instead, we should pay careful attention to and express gratitude for the community we are a part of and are called to serve.

Leadership Center and an Avengers fan) has pointed out to me that "in the movie *Endgame*, what enabled the Avengers to defeat Thanos was their ability to set aside their own egos for the sake of the common good. They fought against Thanos as a genuine team. And then, in one of the biggest shockers of all, Iron Man actually sacrifices himself. However, by the end of the movie, at Iron Man's funeral, you get the sense that for the most part, the heroes are back to their individual lives."

9. Max De Pree, *Leadership Is an Art* (New York: Currency Doubleday, 2004), 11.

Third, participative power is *exercised with vulnerability and trust.*

There is something paradoxical about humanity's creation and mandate. On the one hand, human beings are meant to rule on God's behalf over all creation. On the other hand, they are created uniquely naked and vulnerable. As Andy Crouch observes in his book, "In the primordial moment of blessedness . . . the vice regents of creation were unashamed in their nakedness. *Vulnerability and dignity were not opposed to one another, and neither were dependence and dominion.*"[10]

Paul discovers something similar in his work of leadership. In response to his now-famous "thorn in the flesh," he prays to God for deliverance three times. God responds with words that resonate back to the creation itself: "My power is made perfect in weakness" (2 Cor. 12:9).

Participative power reminds us that power is a consequence of a relationship. Or perhaps more accurately, power is meant to be expressed in partnership. To put it more colloquially still: power is a team sport, not an individual sport. The power (dominion) that human beings are meant to exercise is inherently relational. It is meant to be exercised in vulnerability and dependence upon God, and with vulnerability and dependence on one another. And the relationship at the core of healthy power is between the One who is God and the ones who are made in the image of God.

That interdependence blurs the lines of who exactly is exercising power. In the biblical narrative, God's work and the work of God's people are regularly hard to distinguish. In talking about ancient Israel's conquest of the promised land, the psalmist says this about God's power:

> For not by their own sword did they win the land,
>   nor did their own arm give them victory;

10. Crouch, *Playing God*, 102 (emphasis added).

but your right hand, and your arm,
and the light of your countenance,
for you delighted in them. (Ps. 44:3)

And yet, Israel wasn't a mere bystander in God's work. Israel's work and God's work were inseparably commingled.

Human work was never meant to be done in isolation. From the beginning, our work was intended to be a divine partnership. Perhaps that's why Jesus could speak to his followers in this way: "Come to me, all you that are weary and are carrying heavy burdens, and I will give you rest. Take my yoke upon you, and learn from me; for I am gentle and humble in heart, and you will find rest for your souls. For my yoke is easy, and my burden is light" (Matt. 11:28–30).

For a long time, I pictured Jesus's metaphor of a yoke as though he was a farmer plowing a field, and I was the one wearing the harness and pulling the plow. But the imagery suggests something different. Jesus himself wears the yoke with me, and we are yoked together. And we plow the field together. That's what it means for him to be "gentle and humble in heart," and that's also why his "yoke is easy" and our "burden is light."

Participative power requires us to enter into the work of our followers, to share in carrying the burden of that work. It's easy to reduce the work of leadership to providing direction, giving orders, and holding people accountable for the results. But participative power requires something more. It requires that we share the load. And that can take many forms.

Sometimes that means we help people problem-solve. At other times it means we encourage them to solve the problems on their own. Sometimes it means we come alongside people when they struggle with difficult situations and relationships. At other times it means we give them space to figure out those situations and relationships with others. In each case, we express vulnerability and trust because we are in partnership with them, even as the particular circumstances require a different relational response from us.

DIRECTIVE POWER

I've been a fan of the *Star Trek* franchise since its beginnings. Like many others, I've admired *Star Trek: The Next Generation*'s character, Captain Jean-Luc Picard, for his leadership traits. In the context of discussing the third aspect of healthy power, Picard's command catchphrase, "Make it so!" is memorable shorthand for what I call "directive power."

The fictional character Picard embodies aspects of the two previous kinds of power. Picard uses generative power when he entrusts and empowers his people to do their work without micromanaging. His leadership style is also participative, and he works hard to build a close-knit leadership team, despite his natural reserve. But there are times when directive power is called for, and Captain Picard isn't reluctant to use it. Why might that be?

There are at least three good reasons to use directive power.

First, directive power *provides clarity and focus.*

Not limited to those who command fictional starships, all leaders need to articulate their mission and marshal a community of people to accomplish it. Occasionally, a community discovers the goal and direction together. But more often, someone provides that vision for the community. That vision is an essential characteristic of leadership. In the words of Max De Pree, "The first responsibility of a leader is to define reality."[11]

The metaphor of the human body again is helpful. Each body needs a mechanism for providing direction so the body can function. The brain and nervous system connect and coordinate the different parts of the body to work in unison toward the same goal. So it is with leadership.

But as essential as the brain and nervous system are, they are useless without the rest of the body. In a certain sense, their function is to serve the rest of the body so that the body as a whole can function appropriately. So it is with leadership.

11. De Pree, *Leadership Is an Art*, 11.

And that is why leadership is critical. Directive power provides the clarity and focus essential to the community's creative work. Fundamentally, directive power brings order out of chaos. Just as God spoke order out of primordial chaos, human leadership can use directive speech to shape chaotic contexts into productive work.

Let me return to a previous example. During the 2008 financial crisis, our company faced the gravest challenge to its corporate existence since its founding. Our senior team convened to look at various business options, review our technology pipeline, and consider strategic partnerships or mergers. Lots of alternatives surfaced. Lots of passionate arguments took place. Near the end of our planning work, there was little agreement about what to do next. My task as CEO was to provide clarity and focus. So, I said to my team, "Here is what we are going to do . . ." As Captain Picard might have said, "Make it so."

The gift of power—even directive power—is to serve the mission and the community. Commands can be healthy expressions of power when they provide certainty and direction, a way forward that helps the community to function and to flourish.

Second, directive power *protects the mission and the community.*

Clarity and focus are essential. But what about when external and internal forces threaten the mission or community? How might directive power, including actions seen as coercive, be used in that context?

There is a protective aspect to the power of leadership. In the words of the original mandate to humanity in the garden, we are not only to cultivate the garden but to protect ("keep") it (Gen. 2:15). There are many ways we might do this.

One practical example is dealing with nonperforming members on our team. Of course, we need to provide every opportunity for people to fulfill their responsibilities. And we need to provide kind but honest feedback about their performance in a timely fashion. But sometimes, in the name of being charitable, we refuse to be honest with people (and with ourselves) about their work and their impact on the mission and community of the organization. It is hard to give frank feedback graciously. And it is costly, especially when it creates conflict and tension.

But we don't do anyone any favors by not doing our job as leaders. Even when the other party disagrees with our assessment, part of our task as leaders is to provide our perspective and, in the end, to make the difficult call as to what is best for the organization. Sadly, our inclination to avoid and postpone such conversations only makes things worse.

My friend Jane is a case in point. Jane was head of a nonprofit on whose board I sat. In many ways, she was a great leader. She cared deeply for the organization's mission and the community she led. During a financial downturn, it became clear that the organization needed to combine with another nonprofit to survive. Jane championed the merger with little regard for her own situation and with a singular focus on what was good for the larger community.

Soon after the merger, Jane asked me if she should continue at the company but in a lesser capacity. I was very positive with her because of her stellar work consummating the deal. But I underestimated the difficulty of Jane's transition from the most senior person to "just another" leader. It soon became apparent that it wasn't working out despite her best efforts. I wish I could say that I provided her with honest feedback at that point. But I didn't. I continued to focus on her positive qualities and contributions and ignored the signals that things were going off the rails.

Finally, I told Jane my honest assessment. She was shocked, and rightly so. In the end, I told her, "When you've given your best and it's not enough, it's time to move on." That was hard for her to hear and hard for me to say. And I wish I had been honest enough to say it sooner.

Third, directive power *uses force only when no other options are possible.*

Is the violent use of power ever justified in leadership?

Isaac Asimov is one of my favorite science fiction writers. In his landmark Foundation Series, one of his characters says, "Violence is the last refuge of the incompetent."[12] In other words, people resort to violence when they don't know what else to do. It's a maxim that's both thought provoking and challenging.

But by seeing violence only in negative terms, Asimov simplifies the challenge that the violent use of power poses for those in leadership. What happens if force is necessary to preserve the good and flourishing of creation? Or, as a friend of mine once said, "Sometimes the choice is not between good and bad, but between bad and worse."[13]

Let's go back to my friend Jane. After I finally gave her my honest assessment—and after considerable struggle—Jane concluded that it was time for her to move on. That turned out to be a good decision for the organization and, I think, for her. But what if she hadn't? What if Jane chose to stay and fight?

As with individual life, organizational life is filled with such difficult situations. How do we use power wisely in such a context? Does humility in leadership mean acknowledging we could be wrong and necessarily yielding to the other's point of view?

While there are no simple answers to these kinds of situations, I've found a couple of practices helpful.

For one, the more strongly people react, the more we need to pay close attention to what is going on. People could simply be behaving badly, but we also need to be willing to hear the truth we too quickly dismiss as false. We can not only be wrong, but we can also be culturally blind-sighted. Systemic injustices, such as structural racism and gender inequality, are all too easy to justify as simply "how things are meant to be."

Given the heated nature of these situations, I find it helpful not to react in the moment. Instead, giving myself and others the physical and emotional space and time to act reflectively rather than reactively is always a good idea. Taking that time can also allow us to consult with others who can provide helpful perspectives on the conflict.

---

12. Isaac Asimov, *Foundation* (New York: Octopus Books, 1984), 58.
13. Quote thanks to Steve Brinn.

Another helpful practice is remembering that people are in their roles for a reason, including those of us in leadership. Our job is to serve others, and sometimes that service includes making gut-wrenching decisions that profoundly alter other people's lives. Simply acquiescing to others' passionate fight for what they think is right is not competent leadership. We must listen, learn, and discern.

But in the end, we must also own our responsibility and act in the community's best interest. To quote President Lincoln from his second inaugural address near the end of the American Civil War, we must act "with malice toward none and with charity toward all, with firmness in the right as God gives us to see the right."[14]

Lincoln struggled with the proper use of power, including violence, on a staggering scale that hopefully none of us will ever have to experience. But Lincoln's words help me hold two things together that I find very difficult to reconcile and embody: *love of enemies when those enemies oppose the very good we are called to enact.* In a leadership context, we must make discerning judgments and live with the consequences of our decisions.

In summary, healthy models of power span a range of possible expressions. In the first instance, power is intended to be expressed generously to create time and space for others to exercise their own power. Much as parents allow their adult children to come into their own, God's creatures are allowed to exercise their gifts and abilities (their "powers") in ways distinct and unique to them.

In the second instance, power is intended to be expressed personally, with empathy and compassion. And with a willingness to share in the consequences of failure.

Finally, power is designed to be expressed directly, to provide purpose and direction, and to constrain and restrain what is not good in the pursuit of our mission and in support of our communities.

---

14. "Lincoln's Second Inaugural Address," National Park Service, accessed June 13, 2023, https://www.nps.gov/linc/learn/historyculture/lincoln-second -inaugural.htm.

God is remarkably patient and even reluctant to use the last kind of power, particularly when it requires coercion. That's a wise practice we do well to emulate.

A LITTLE CHAOS

Kate Winslet, Alan Rickman, and Stan Tucci are three of my favorite actors. All three are found in a not-so-well-known movie entitled *A Little Chaos*. The film tells a fictional story of the creation of Louis XIV's monumental garden of Versailles. I visited Versailles several years ago, and must say the gardens there are stunning to this day, even to a nongardener like me.

In the movie, King Louis's royal landscape architect, charged with creating the most magnificent gardens imaginable, looks for the best landscape designers in the realm. He settles on several, including one who was an unconventional choice, a woman known for her eccentric designs. Played wonderfully by Kate Winslet, she delivers remarkable results for her royal patron.

When she asks the royal landscape architect why he was willing to take a chance on her and her unconventional methods, he responds with the most memorable line in the movie: "These gardens should be large enough to embrace forces other than my own."

That line not only expresses a willingness to exercise power with a spirit of humility, but it also captures the distinctive character of generative power: creating space (and perhaps some resulting chaos) for the exercise and flourishing of powers other than our own.

HIDDEN IN PLAIN SIGHT

We are easily seduced by the dramatic and the spectacular. Power is often wielded for dramatic effect and in pursuit of spectacular results. Jesus himself was not immune to these temptations, as the gospel record reminds us (Matt. 4:1–11; Luke 4:1–13). It's interesting, therefore, to note the circumstance and appearance of Jesus at his resurrection.

Lavinia Fontana was a remarkable Renaissance painter who was also one of the first career female artists in western Europe. Danielle Carrabino, Italian Renaissance and baroque art scholar, says this about her: "Fontana is often considered to be the first woman artist of the Renaissance to be working on par with male artists of her day, thanks to her prolific output as well as the high prices her art fetched."* In contrast to Kate Winslet's fictional character and story, Lavinia was a real person.

In her piece, *Noli Me Tangere*,** she painted the resurrection encounter between Jesus and Mary Magdalene recorded in John's Gospel. In the account, Mary mistakes Jesus for an ordinary gardener. Instead of the grand entrance one might have expected after being resurrected from the dead, Jesus's appearance is singularly understated. Fontana wonderfully imagines and captures the ordinary appearance of Jesus in her painting.

As leaders, it isn't easy to be content with being ordinary. We all want to be exceptional. But as Jesus reminded his disciples regarding their spiritual practices, God "sees" and "is in secret" (Matt. 6:4, 6). The original phrase translated as "in secret" is the source of the English word "encrypted." It's not a stretch to suggest that God's good works are in that sense "encrypted" in the ordinary circumstances of our lives. And that God sees what is "encrypted" in our ordinary work.

We tend to keep looking for God in the extraordinary or spectacular. But the goodness of the everyday is where God's power is hidden in plain sight. We shouldn't be surprised when that's true for us as well.

* Danielle Carrabino, "Lavinia Fontana: Renaissance Artist," SCMA, December 5, 2019, https://scma.smith.edu/blog/lavinia-fontana-renaissance-artist.

** Lavinia Fontana, *Noli Me Tangere*, 1581, available at https://depree.org/wise -leader/image-8.

5

Wisdom and Healthy Practices of Power

Given a healthy vision of power, how do we develop healthy practices of power? What might it look like for us as leaders to
relate well with the people we serve and with the organizations we
are called to lead? Perhaps most challenging, what practices do we
need to cultivate a healthy leadership style that mitigates the toxic
allure of the misuse and abuse of power?

Practices Related to Those We Lead

Leadership insulates. An invisible barrier forms around us when we
become leaders. The more senior the role we assume, the more insular
the bubble becomes.

There are good reasons for that bubble to form. When organizational demands overwhelm us as leaders, we create administrative
teams and management technologies to screen out unnecessary distractions. This allows us to establish an insular space to do our work
effectively and efficiently. That is the benefit of the bubble.

But there are unintended side effects. People begin to communicate more circumspectly with us. We lose touch with those we are
called to lead and serve. Getting a sense of the reality on the ground
becomes more challenging. If we are not careful, we can be misled
and mislead others.

So, what can we do?

We can begin by acknowledging that the privileges of leadership tempt us to stay in our bubble and enjoy our leadership perks. They can be quite intoxicating: an office with a door we can shut, an administrative assistant who vigilantly screens our visitors and guards our time, as well as a dedicated team who carry out our vision and strategies.

There is a godlike quality to leadership that can be hard to resist. If we are not careful, we can believe that these are ours by right and exist to serve us.

I have seen this happen in my own work. And I have seen various leaders succumb to the same temptation. Sadly, those who serve in organizations with explicitly Christian commitments seem most vulnerable. The combination of divine purpose and an insular leadership bubble rarely ends well. Acknowledging that temptation and our capacity for self-deception is an excellent place to start.

But that's not enough. We need to find practical ways to break out of the bubble and reconnect with the people whom we are called to serve.

Bursting the Leadership Bubble

To begin with, you need to be present to the people in your organization. There are many ways to do this. A simple one is making regular time in your schedule to share a meal or a cup of coffee. This can begin with the immediate team that reports to you. If you are an agenda-driven person, as I am, it may take a good deal of work to keep the conversation from devolving into just another work meeting. Being present to another person is hard work, but it's a leadership skill that can be learned.

In larger organizations, it's impossible to do this with everyone. Still, it's helpful to find a few people with whom you can engage so you can see and hear what others are experiencing.

One of wisdom's most countercultural leadership insights is to pay attention to those who are furthest from the center of power. From the beginning, the wisdom from above teaches the importance of concern for the powerless. In ancient Israel, these were the widow, the orphan, and the resident alien.[1] Culturally, these people had no social or economic power. And yet God expected leaders to listen to them.

Transposing that into a modern corporate context, we need to pay attention to people with little or no organizational power. In my experience, it isn't easy to hear what those people have to say, and it's not easy for them to say what we need to hear. That's particularly so when systemic issues have been long ignored. In that case, it's good to bring in some outside help.

For a season, I stepped out of the day-to-day operations of my company. I had other interests, including spending more time with my family and serving on several nonprofit boards. For a few years, things went well. But then I noticed that the company was losing its creative edge, so I started investing more time to listen.

What I found puzzled me. Most people continued to give me upbeat assessments about what was going on. Finally, I decided to bring in a consulting company to assess our corporate culture. I wanted them to do a deep dive to figure out what was happening. And I encouraged the employees to be brutally honest with them.

I still remember the dinner I had with the consultants after they had completed their preliminary conversations. After some initial pleasantries, an uncomfortable silence hung in the air. Finally, I said, "What do you need to tell me that you think I don't want to hear?"

They told me that our creative stagnation was the result of leadership practices that stifled innovation and felt oppressive to many. And those practices had developed because I had stopped paying attention. That was tough for me to hear. And I knew that was very hard for people to say. Thankfully, that hard truth helped us make needed changes and set a different course forward.

---

1. For example, see Robert Alter's comments on Exod. 22:21–22 and Deut. 10:17–19, in Alter, *The Hebrew Bible*, vol. 1 (New York: Norton, 2019), 307 and 655–66, respectively.

Learning to hear well is difficult. As the apostle James counsels, "Be quick to listen, slow to speak, slow to anger" (James 1:19). Defensiveness and anger surface surprisingly quickly. I know because I've reacted that way more times than I care to admit, although thankfully not at that dinner. The conversation can be over before it begins. And the danger grows proportionally with the conviction of the rightness of one's organizational cause and leadership practices.

That's why humility and power must always be held together.

Balancing Mission and Community

Wise leaders use power for the sake of others. Sadly, even when we are concerned for others, we can focus on the results our organization produces to the exclusion of the well-being of the people who make up that organization. One of the most significant challenges we face as leaders is holding together our responsibility for both *mission* and *community*. Both matter.

In ancient times, shepherds were metaphors for leaders. That image provides a helpful corrective to our perception of the leader's work. First of all, being seen as shepherds reminds us that our responsibilities include tending to followers. Followers are persons who have value in and of themselves and are not merely a means to an end. Even when that end is as important as the organization's mission, leaders remain responsible for the people who follow them.

Also, being a shepherd is unglamorous work. In the ancient world, shepherds were essential workers who were grossly undervalued. They did the dirty and difficult job of watching over and caring for animals not known for their cooperation. Perhaps for that reason, the image of the shepherd reminds ancients and moderns alike that leadership can involve caring for difficult people in uncomfortable situations.

Psalm 23 provides a vivid description of God as our shepherd. For that reason, it is one of the most well-known and beloved of all the psalms. It also provides us with an example of what great leaders do.

A quick review of Psalm 23 through that lens is instructive.[2] Wise leaders will:

1. Provide what followers need to flourish in their work ("I lack nothing").
2. Ensure that followers' hard work can be balanced with time and space for rest and renewal ("He makes me lie down in green pastures, / he leads me beside quiet waters, / he refreshes my soul").
3. Direct their followers on what constitutes good work ("He guides me along the right paths") that is consistent with the character of the organization ("for his name's sake").
4. Use their power ("your rod and your staff") to guide and protect followers through dangerous times and circumstances ("the darkest valley").
5. Create hospitable spaces and places ("you prepare a table before me") for followers to feel valued and appreciated ("you anoint my head with oil; / my cup overflows") in their work, even in inhospitable circumstances ("in the presence of my enemies").

Ensuring that both our organization's mission and its community not only survive but thrive is difficult. Sometimes, these concerns are in tension with one another. Focusing on one can lead to the detriment of the other. Wisdom requires discernment to know how to balance the two.

At my software company, we practiced eating Friday lunches together. Nearly all of us spent our time at workstations, heads down, doing the hard work of developing and testing the latest software releases. While there were times of interaction, most were driven by business concerns. That was why we started providing and eating Friday lunches together.

Friday lunch was a chance to see other people and interact differently. People had an opportunity to talk about their own lives,

2. Following quotes are from the NIV.

families, and other interests. Some spent the lunch hour taking walks together or playing cards. It was a chance to be part of a community of people and not simply be a cog in a machine that produced software. It humanized our work.

During an economic downturn, we were faced with cutting back on our operating expenses. One option was to cut funding for our Friday lunches. After all, some argued, they were not mission-critical. But after eliminating them for a few weeks, we knew we had lost something vital. So we decided to reinstitute Friday lunches. "Preparing a table" for our team turned out to be essential after all.

The Importance of Cadence in Our Work

Balancing a commitment to work with intensity, on the one hand, with a commitment to rest and renewal, on the other, is challenging. During our start-up phase, I recruited a young software engineer from MIT for an on-site interview. She was exceptionally bright and deeply committed to her work. In many ways, she seemed like an ideal fit. Everyone who interviewed her gave her an enthusiastic thumbs-up. When I met with her to extend an offer, to my surprise, she graciously declined. So, I asked her why.

She said that she loved our work but felt like we didn't have the intensity she was looking for. As we talked further, she clarified that she was looking for a company that expected 24/7 commitment from their people. In contrast, I told her early in our interview that we were committed to work-life balance even in a start-up context. We believed that taking the long view was important. We acknowledged that people wanted and needed space and time outside of work to be effective. So I told her that even though I was sad to lose her, I realized her work culture expectations didn't fit ours.

Highly motivated individuals and high-performance organizations can easily confuse relentless work with a commitment to work with intensity for great results. And finding the right cadence for our work becomes more complicated as technology blurs the boundaries between work and home. As those margins become less well marked, is it surprising that we as leaders (and those who follow us) become less effective at finding space and time to rest?

As leaders, we need to pay attention to the example we set for those who follow us. In our desire to be a role model of hard work, we can inadvertently create an institutional culture that glorifies relentless work. My friend Rod Wilson, formerly president of Regent College in Canada, was a good case in point.

As board chair of Regent College, I saw up close Rod's commitment to his work. He loved Regent, expected a great deal of himself, and was committed to setting an example of service to the Regent community. While Rod often worked past midnight and on weekends, he was always gracious with those who reported to him. He regularly encouraged them to take the time they needed for vacations and family even as he expected considerably more of himself.

A few years into our relationship, I had a conversation with him about his leadership practice. We talked about the unintended consequences and the implicit expectations it set for everyone else. And we explored the possibility of adopting a healthier work cadence.

Despite being at the end of a demanding capital campaign, Rod acted. He decided to go to Wales for two months that summer, to a small village that had no Internet connections. After he returned, he started practicing a regular twenty-four-hour Saturday Sabbath. As Rod told me later, it felt like a detox experience. But it transformed his life and leadership.[3]

Accountability and Different Kinds of Failure

Perhaps no issue is more difficult in balancing mission and community than dealing with accountability and failure. Responsibility has to do with delivering results consistent with our mission. Accountability is not only necessary because of its immediate results but because of its effects on the broader organization.

3. Personal communication with Rod Wilson.

Allowing people not to be accountable undermines the fabric of the community and compromises its mission. Simply put, we are derelict in our duty as leaders if we de-emphasize accountability.

And yet we are faced with the reality of failure. How should we think about it? How might we hold people accountable when failure occurs? I find it helpful to think about three types of failures.

First, some failures are due to inexperience. Responsible parents would not demand their children learn to walk without ever falling. As human beings, we learn by doing, with plenty of mistakes made along the way. The role of a parent is in part to provide appropriate learning experiences for a child to grow and develop. That's a helpful metaphor for dealing with failures of the first kind. Wise leaders discern appropriate assignments for inexperienced people and structure accountability as learning experiences. As with responsible parents, we do not protect our followers from the consequences of their actions, even as we take steps to protect the organizations and them from serious harm.

Second, even experienced people fail. These situations are more complicated. For example, sometimes people are mismatched with their roles. Either the role evolves into responsibilities for which they are no longer suited, or they are placed in a role that is unsuited to them. As leaders, we need to discern carefully about people and the assignments they are given.

One of my best senior engineers was a good case in point. Not only was he a terrific technologist, but he had a great way with people, both with customers and with developers. As a result, when the opportunity came, I promoted him to lead the largest part of our product development team. At the time, it seemed a great fit to both of us. But we soon discovered that his real love was software development and not managing complex relational dynamics. So we restructured his role to focus on his sweet spot.

Third, some failures are deliberate. The possibility of a malicious act by a bad actor in an organization is a sad reality of life. Although everyone deserves the presumption of innocence, when guilt is proven, we need to act, as unpleasant as that may be. Protecting the organization's mission and community requires us to safeguard the common good.

Creating Space for Dealing with Failures

But accountability is much more than simply doling out consequences for failures. And the biblical witness provides rich insight into this area.

To begin with, we must learn to admit our failures. As human beings, we are especially adept at avoidance and denial. And that is true whether we are leaders or followers. As I mentioned earlier, I would much rather give positive feedback to my team than deal with their poor performance. Coming to terms with others' inadequacies is hard to do.

One of the challenges of leadership is creating appropriate space for people to acknowledge them.

As a small step in that direction, I always keep a box of Kleenex in my office. And I make it a point to let people know that they can talk about their challenges with me. I will never forget the day a team member sat in my office describing a complex set of conflicted organizational relationships. As she shared her struggles, she began to cry. "I hate it when women cry at work!" she said with tears running down her cheeks. I offered her my box of Kleenex. She smiled when I said, "I seem to have that effect on people in my office."

Allowing people to face their failures and taking the time to hear their admission is a skill we need to learn as leaders. Of course, we are neither therapists nor priests. But we need to create space and time to deal with failure constructively if we expect genuine accountability. Because, in the end, accountability is about personal ownership of our own responsibilities. Hiding from and not dealing with the root causes of our failures is problematic both for the individual and for the community.

Personally, I find it easier to move on rather than to deal with personal and institutional inadequacies. There are times when a simple acknowledgment is all that is necessary. But other times, particularly when there are unhealthy personal or institutional patterns, we need to take more time to reflect.

The biblical practice of confession—seemingly remote from modern business—is a helpful way to bring our failures into the light, face them squarely, and ask for help to make them right. The wisdom of the ancient sages says it clearly:

> No one who conceals transgressions will prosper,
>> but one who confesses and forsakes them will obtain
>> mercy. (Prov. 28:13)

As leaders, we are charged with both carrying out our organization's mission and caring for our organization's people. To do each well, we need to deal wisely with failures. Do we simply jettison people who do not perform? No. Do we merely ignore failures in hopes they will be self-correcting? Of course not.

Neither approach is responsible, much less wise leadership. It takes courage to face our individual and collective responsibilities, courage on our part as leaders, and courage on the part of our followers. Creating space for that is an important aspect of creating a culture where that courage is rewarded. As we do, we will discover the truth of the remarkable promise: "Mercy triumphs over judgment" (James 2:13).

Practices Related to the Organizations We Lead

Every organization engages in some form of strategic planning. That process is often framed as imagining what the world might look like five, ten, or even twenty years out. That kind of planning raises questions that can help shape its work in the present.

But what if your horizon were a hundred years? What kind of questions might you ask then? Perhaps one of the first questions is: Why would anyone want to look that far out?

The MARS Corporation—perhaps best known for making M&Ms—has thought about these questions. My friend Steve Garber is a senior advisor to the company. He has been gracious enough to share some of their thoughts with me.

Why would a company like MARS care about such things? Like every other for-profit company, it cares about near-term financial results. But MARS concluded that sustained profitability requires a more complex bottom line and a much longer planning horizon.

One of MARS's business issues is the availability of cocoa beans used to make chocolate. The idea of a hundred-year planning horizon came out of discussions around the long-term viability of the supply chain for cocoa beans. What business ecosystem would be needed to supply those beans into the indefinite future—say, one hundred years from now? What structural changes need to be made to the relationship between MARS and its suppliers to create a sustainable future for both? The concept of "the economics of mutuality" came from that question, which reimagines business as a long-term, mutually beneficial structure rather than as a series of self-serving transactions.[4]

Such thinking is rare in organizations and seems impractical, perhaps even foolhardy. As a businessperson, I understand the sentiment. The pressures of generating results of all kinds—successful product launches, hockey-stick growth, significant profits—make focus and clarity about the near term essential. The same is true in nonprofit and religious organizations, even though the particulars are different. "What have you done for me lately?" is as common a refrain in those worlds as in the for-profit world. But as I will argue in the next chapter, wise leaders need "bifocal vision," the capacity to focus both on what's immediately in front of them and on what is far off. Both are essential to wisdom.

And taking the long view applies to looking backward as well as forward. Some issues are consequences of long-ignored problems, deeply embedded in how we do things. Changing organizational cul-

4. Personal conversation with Steve Garber.

ture—that is, making structural changes—is problematic because it's hard to see the problem. Structural issues often present themselves as "this is just the way things are." It takes considerable insight and even courage to see problems clearly. And sometimes, it takes a crisis to make structural change unavoidable.

Our recent societal reckoning with systemic racism is a case in point. For many non-Black Americans, systemic racism seemed like something we solved decades ago. A few years back, I heard a White pastor say in a sermon: "I thought we dealt with all this in the 1960s ... but I guess we didn't." Indeed not. The video of George Floyd being suffocated to death by a White policeman brought searing clarity to a systemic issue many thought was a relic of the past.

For many non-Black Americans, racism is an individual problem, not a systemic one. But the recent racial crises provoked many, myself included, to reflect on the role of structural evil in our national history. During that time, I read two beneficial books, *The Color of Compromise* by Jemar Tisby and *White Too Long* by Robert P. Jones. Tisby, who is Black, and Jones, who is White, researched and documented the history of racism in the United States, including the support of evangelical theology and practice.

The books were hard for me to read. Even harder was coming to terms with my lack of awareness of the issue and my participation in structures that benefit me at the expense of my Black brothers and sisters.

Structural issues have profound, long-term, deep implications in our world. That's why wise leaders have to care about and attend to them. The way we do that is through "institutional thinking."

Caring about Institutions

At a recent gathering with senior Christian leaders, I heard one say, "What matters is people. Institutions don't matter. There are no institutions in heaven." If he is correct, then what I'm about to say is a waste of time. But I believe his vision is too narrow.

Institutions seem to have a bad reputation, and not just among some Christians. For many of us, the word "institution" conjures up images of an oppressive and inflexible bureaucracy. It seems the opposite of the adaptive and innovative organizations that everyone aspires to in the twenty-first century. Who then would want to be caught dead doing institutional thinking? Perhaps only those already institutionalized!

It seems a dark word to be using today. But I hope to persuade you that "there is still good" in a concept that many would more associate with Darth Vader than with Luke Skywalker!

Institutions are a way of talking about human structures that transcend the individual. At their best, they are "the way the teeming abundance of human creativity and culture are handed on to future generations."[5]

There are many examples—family, schools, government, for-profit and nonprofit corporations, just to name a few. They provide a way for our life and work to contribute not only to the present but also to the future.

For better or worse, institutions embody our legacy as leaders. For example, both vices and virtues propagate from one generation to another in our families. That's not a surprise to those familiar with the biblical narrative. From the beginning, moral consequences extended well past individuals. God visited

> "the iniquity of the parents
> upon the children
> and the children's children,
> to the third and the fourth generation." (Exod. 34:7)

Likewise, so do virtues:

---

5. Andy Crouch, *Playing God: Redeeming the Gift of Power* (Downers Grove, IL: InterVarsity Press, 2013), 188.

Happy are those who fear the LORD,
who greatly delight in his commandments.
Their descendants will be mighty in the land;
the generation of the upright will be blessed. (Ps. 112:1–2)

All this raises the stakes for our work as leaders. Leadership is not just a season of performance with a team of people. Leadership inevitably contributes to—again, for better or worse—the creation of institutions. Or destroying them. Wise leaders pay attention not only to the immediate results of their actions but also to the long-term structural consequences. A healthy institution is the legacy of a wise leader.

Embodying Healthy Institutional Power

Institutional power is never distributed equally. By its very nature, being a leader involves having more power than those being led. That's why leadership is so easily subverted into an exercise of power to the detriment of others. As we have already seen, humility is the essential virtue of leadership whereby our power is held in check.

Given that unequal power is a fact of institutional life, what are signs that such power dynamics are healthy?

First, the more power one has, the more critical a spirit of humility becomes. Power is intoxicating. And coming into power can be a dangerous season, particularly when it happens quickly. Every one of us is susceptible to pride and arrogance.

When I first became an executive with an internal technology start-up within the Weyerhaeuser Company, I found it incredibly exciting. We were developing cutting-edge, point-of-sale, virtual-reality design technology, getting great national press and attention, and received terrific support from our senior leaders. Everything was going our way. I felt like all of my gifts and abilities were in full flow. It was heady stuff.

In the middle of all that, one day, a close friend took me aside. She said she noticed—how did she put it?—oh yes, now I remember—that I was starting to act like a jerk. That brought me up short. What in the world could she mean? I thought I was still the same person—the same kind, thoughtful, humble person I always had been. But evidently not!

She saw something happening that I could not see. As success and power expanded in my life, my ego grew along with them. Although I doubted it at the time, she was a good friend to tell me what no one else was willing to say. Her words punctured my inflated self, which had begun to act with hubris and arrogance.

I have to admit that it was easy to dismiss her feedback at the moment. I thought she was critical because she was envious of my success. As the saying goes, it's easy to shoot the messenger. But in retrospect, I'm grateful for her honest feedback and her willingness to risk our friendship by providing it. It has stood for me as a reminder of the danger of increasing power without a proportionate increase in a spirit of humility.

The second characteristic of a healthy institutional power dynamic is that flourishing is widely distributed. All parts of the organization need to flourish, not just the leader. In one sense, that's simply a corollary of Jesus's mandate that leadership is about service. If we serve others well, then they should flourish. Conversely, if others are not flourishing and we are, that's a sign that something is amiss. Power is to be used for the benefit of others, not just for ourselves.

While this is easy to say in theory, it can be very complicated in practice. And sometimes, the best of intentions leads to the worst of complications. Let me give an example.

There are seasons in institutional life when an institution's survival is at stake. The pressures of such times can bring out the worst in leaders. Fear and anxiety can distort our responses to crises, bringing character-related leadership issues to the surface.

This is particularly true in religious institutions. When an organization that claims to do God's work is in peril, some will do anything necessary to save it. I've spent much of my adult life working in governance with theological schools and churches. Almost everyone

I've worked alongside has been deeply committed to their mission. Yet, more often than one might expect, crises trigger a well-intended response that causes serious damage.

One situation involved a congregation that needed redevelopment. Like many mainline churches, it had failed to attract people in their thirties and forties. So, the church brought in a young, dynamic pastor who was tasked with changing the status quo. The pastor, along with other leaders in the church, decided to make significant changes to the worship and life of the church. Without a doubt, many of the changes were necessary.

What proved fatal was how it was done. To preserve the institution's viability, power was wielded that brooked no opposition. Everything and everyone that opposed change was condemned. Everything and everyone that supported change was deemed good. Many left the church. Unsurprisingly, after a time, so did the pastor.

There was little question about the ends that the church leaders were trying to achieve. The fact that the changes were vital for long-term viability made those means easy to rationalize. Surely some personal and even communal sacrifice was necessary to accomplish God's mission in the world.

It's far too easy to use Jesus's language about being persecuted for righteousness' sake to justify poor leadership practices. In the end, the dead giveaway was the abuse of power. When it is used to browbeat followers into submission, something is wrong.

Becoming Trustees of Institutions

Given the importance of institutions, how should we relate to them? Andy Crouch uses the word "trustee" to describe the critical role of those who lead by serving. His use of the word shouldn't be confused with the few who do governance work, as in a "board of trustees."

Anyone can be a trustee in Crouch's sense, including those with little or no formal leadership roles. He argues that trustees are those who "have seen, and borne, the worst that institutions can do—and yet they have somehow escaped the abyss of cynicism. Instead they enter into the life of their institutions, embodying a better way, bearing the institution's pain and offering hope."[6]

Healthy institutions need good trustees at all levels. In keeping with Jesus's vision of leadership, trustees are servants who bear the institution's pain and offer hope. That's a tall order, particularly for those of us who have seen, in Otto von Bismarck's vivid metaphor, "how the sausage is made."

Consequently, an aspect of being a good trustee is learning how to bear the burdens of an institution's pain without being destroyed by it. Making the distinction between burdens we are to carry and burdens that others are to carry is essential. Not every institutional problem is ours to bear.

But there remains the problem of what to do with the pain of dissonance between what we hope for and our present reality. That disparity is the source of pain because of our love for the institution. And the greater our passion and commitment, the greater our experience of dissonance and pain.

This is where wise spiritual guides and poets can help us. As T. S. Eliot reminds us, we need to learn to "not care" as well as to care. Caring too much can be a problem. Cultivating an appropriate sense of detachment is an essential characteristic of wise leadership. To quote Eliot again:

> This is the use of memory:
> For liberation—not less of love but expanding
> Of love beyond desire, and so liberation
> From the future as well as the past.[7]

Our focus on an expected future can, ironically, impair our ability to care for our institutions in the present and to offer genuine hope.

---

6. Crouch, *Playing God*, 217.

7. T. S. Eliot, "Little Gidding," in *The Complete Poems and Plays, 1909–1950* (New York: Harcourt Brace, 1980), 142.

Our desires for specific outcomes can distort our love into something unhelpful, even destructive. Wisely, Eliot encourages us toward a detachment that enables our love to expand "beyond desire, and so [liberating us] from the future as well as the past."

PRACTICES RELATED TO OURSELVES AS LEADERS

One of the gifts of being human is that we have limits. We are finite images of the infinite God. Beyond that, we are broken creatures. Each of us is compromised in our ability to represent a wholly good God. As such, we are not promising vessels for God's power and grace to the world.

That's something Moses had learned by the time he encountered God at the burning bush in the wilderness of Sinai.[8] After his remarkable adoption as a baby by Pharaoh's daughter and education as a prince of Egypt, he tried to effect his own version of deliverance for his people in slavery. One day, he killed an Egyptian for beating one of his Hebrew kinfolk. His instinct for justice was admirable, but—as he quickly discovered from both Pharaoh's and his own people's reactions—he was in over his head. Neither the immediate need, a personal desire to make things right, nor even a royal position from which to make a difference was enough. Something more was necessary.

Learning to wield power well requires discipline. Moses's forty years in the Sinai wilderness—strangely parallel to Israel's own forty-year experience in the wilderness—was one long lesson in humility and discipline. The prince of Egypt, exiled by Pharaoh and the Hebrew people, tended sheep. As I observed earlier, being a shepherd was one of the most menial jobs in the ancient world. Day after day, month after month, decade after decade, Moses was learning the discipline of caring for creatures not known for their wisdom and insight, as a person who himself lacked wisdom and insight. No

8. For the details of this story of Moses, see Exod. 2 and 3.

wonder Moses's humility was on full display when God finally met him at the burning bush.

What can we learn from Moses's experience? I suspect none of us will spend forty years in a literal wilderness. Nevertheless, learning the limits of our humanity, including facing our own brokenness, is essential for the wise use of power.

Thankfully, there are practices that help shape us to that end. I call these "*the practices of finitude.*" In other words, these practices remind and form us in ways that acknowledge our limitations.

We will now look at three such practices: sleep, solitude, and sabbath.

The Discipline of Sleep

I used to do my best work late at night. With a young family and a demanding career, I often worked long after my kids and spouse were in bed. I have to admit that I enjoyed the uninterrupted time. No coworkers needed help with their projects. No kids interrupted my train of thought. I got a lot done. Still, staying up later and later to do more and more work became a problem.

I discovered that I was not alone. Numerous sleep experts have noted with considerable alarm the growing problem of sleep deprivation in our culture (for a sampler, just Google "sleep deprivation"). The demands of a competitive economy increase expectations of personal job performance, including the time we spend on work. All of it takes a significant toll on the amount of sleep we get.

In Psalm 3, we are invited to imagine David praying during one of the darkest days of his reign as king of Israel. In that context, I find it remarkable that he says, "I lie down and sleep" (v. 5). Frankly, that seems a bit odd to me. Why would David sleep in a crisis? And, even if he needed to sleep, why would that be important enough for him to work into his prayer? Isn't sleep merely a necessity that gets in the way of our leadership work?

Evidently, it wasn't for David. The psalmist reminds us that sleep is an expression of faith. Our biological need for rest is a built-in reminder from our Creator that we are finite. Leadership can create the illusion that we are in control of the outcomes of our work. Our culture reinforces this illusion by projecting onto leaders almost god-like expectations.

In contrast, a healthy vision of leadership recognizes the importance of human agency but understands its limitations. In the end, it is God who sustains us and our work. So, David got it right. "I lie down and sleep" is first and foremost an expression of faith in the God who is at work in all of our work.

Further, David reminds us that sleep is an expression of resistance. Fear drives much of our contemporary sleeplessness. Fear of failure. Fear of looking bad. Fear of disappointing others. Fear of losing our leadership role. The list goes on and on.

David also had much to fear. When his son Absalom successfully engineered a political coup, David's life was literally on the line. Consider verse 6 of the psalm:

> I am not afraid of tens of thousands of people
> who have set themselves against me all around.

In that context, his choice to sleep is not only an act of faith but also an act of resistance to the fear that resulted from his circumstances. My natural response to fear is to work harder. This psalm reminds us that rest is as essential an act of resistance to fear as is work.

Finally, sleep is God's means for the renewal of our work. "I wake again, for the LORD sustains me" (v. 5). Sleep revitalizes us for the tasks for which we are responsible. We ignore our biological need for sleep at our peril. Not only does sleep deprivation have long-term health effects, but we have all seen its effects on the quality of our work.

Sleep acknowledges the limits of our creatureliness. We discover in times of crises that we can't be "like God" after all. But we can with David learn to say,

> I lie down and sleep;
>   I wake again, for the LORD sustains me.

We can learn to experience sleep as an act of faith and trust in God rather than ourselves.

As leaders, we sometimes believe that if we don't do something, nothing will happen. I often felt that way when starting my own business with limited staff and resources. Nevertheless, particularly at such times, learning to stop and sleep is a profound act of faith and trust in God. Of course, we have an essential part to play in the work God has entrusted to us. But perhaps our most important work is an expression of our inability to do what God alone can do. Sleep expresses our confidence that God will do what we cannot. As I wrote in one of my journals many years ago,

> What if more is needed?
> What if what I have is not enough?
> Limits bring us to the
> edge of faith—
>   faith's possibilities
> at cliff's edge.
> Limits mark where
> God begins and we end.[9]

The Discipline of Sabbath

It is strange how we turn our vices into virtues. We've turned what was intended to be life-giving (something that lies behind our word

9. Uli Chi, *Life in the Intersection* (Seattle: Self-published, 2011), 11.

for "virtue") into something vicious (a term that has the same root as our word "vice").[10] In modern Western culture, relentless work is viewed as a badge of honor. I've worked in organizations where people measure their commitment by how long they are prepared to work and how much they are ready to sacrifice. People skip lunches, miss family vacations, and break promises to neighbors and friends to focus on their work. And by the way, lest you think this is a rant against others, I've done all those things myself. Just ask my work colleagues, family, and friends.

In our relentless, 24/7 world, God offers the gift of Sabbath. We can get off the hamster wheel of restless work one day a week. On that day, we can take time to reflect on what we are doing and why. And we can stop to enjoy the work that we have done. At least, that's God's intention for human beings. As Jesus himself said, "The sabbath was made for humankind" (Mark 2:27).

Ironically, Israel's slavery in Egypt—the ultimate in 24/7 commitment!—is replicated in our unbounded commitment to work. Except now, we do it willingly rather than by compulsion. At least, that is true for some of us. Much as Pharaoh used fear and anxiety to intimidate the Jewish people into submission, fear and anxiety drive much of our restless and relentless work. In contrast, as Walter Brueggemann notes in his book *Sabbath as Resistance*: "Divine rest on the seventh day of creation [on which the sabbath practice is modeled] has made clear (a) that [God] is not a workaholic, (b) that [God] is not anxious about the full functioning of creation, and (c) that the well-being of creation does not depend on endless work."[11]

Even sadder and more ironic, in the history of both Jewish and Christian practice, the Sabbath has on occasion been turned from a liberating command into an oppressive obligation. But Brueggemann's book title suggests the true purpose of the Sabbath: resistance

---

10. My thanks to Steve Garber for pointing this out.

11. Walter Brueggemann, *Sabbath as Resistance* (Louisville: Westminster John Knox, 2014), 6.

to a way of life that is oppressive to what it means to be human. And that is as important in the twenty-first century as it was millennia ago when Israel was liberated from its bondage in Egypt. Perhaps more so now.

One of the great questions of the twenty-first century is whether human beings are (or should be) seen merely as machines. Into that debate, the ancient Sabbath command speaks a wise warning. Human beings are made in the incomparable image and likeness of God, one that should not be reduced to or treated like anything else.

The Sabbath is an essential reminder of who we are and whose we are. Particularly in this century, we must resist the assumption that being human is merely a matter of biological mechanisms and that, therefore, we can treat human beings like machines. The Sabbath is a weekly reminder that we are more than what we do, as important as our work is. We are called to stop, look up, and—as God does— "rejoice in [our] works" (Ps. 104:31).

In one way, Sabbath is intended for our workweek the way sleep is designed for our workday. It is an intentional reminder of our limits as human beings. It is an act of faith, as is going to sleep each night, that the world and our work can be entrusted into God's care. And that God is at work even when we are not. In one sense, that's easier when we are unconsciously asleep than when we are consciously awake. Our minds can be preoccupied with all that isn't getting done while "resting" on the Sabbath. That's certainly been true in my experience. Resting turns out not to be so easy after all.

In addition to stopping my everyday work, another element of the Sabbath is changing the focus of my attention. Instead of merely zeroing in on my productive work, Sabbath reminds me that life is about relationships.

In Jewish practice, a significant part of the day is time spent with family, enjoying their company, and delighting in life together. That suggests playing games, going for a walk, and even cooking a meal together. The practice of Sabbath is not just work stoppage. It elevates our sights to see why we are working and takes time to delight in the goodness of creation. As the apostle Paul says, God has provided us "with everything for our enjoyment" (1 Tim. 6:17).

To say it slightly differently, Sabbath is when work should be or become play. I find my Sabbath times most life-giving when I'm not worried so much about what I am doing as I am about how I am doing it. Even things that I (or others) might consider work, if done with delight and a sense of playfulness, seem to be in keeping with Sabbath intentions. That's especially true if it represents a change of routine from what I've been doing during the rest of the week.

HENRY'S OFF-BROADWAY

Early in my career, I was on a fast track at the Weyerhaeuser Company's R&D division and also working on a PhD in computer science. For several years, I was juggling a growing young family, graduate course work, and a more-than-full-time professional career. In many ways, it was insanity, but such is youth's imagined capacity and naivete.

It was one of the most stressful times of my long marriage with Gayle. One time, I remember sitting in a car in a parking lot with her when she told me she couldn't keep going the way we were. I knew she carried most of the burden of family life even as I was preoccupied with my work and studies. Nevertheless, her words shocked me to my senses, which was a very good thing.

Life was so busy that we rarely had time to connect. But as a result of our conversation, we decided to take every Friday evening for just the two of us. We hired a babysitter for our two little kiddos and went to a Seattle restaurant called Henry's Off-Broadway. Henry's had a bar with live piano music where we sat for three hours each week, talked, and had appetizers and drinks. (Money was an issue back then, so dinners out were not an option. Appetizers were all we could afford.)

Sitting at a bar, having wine and Pepsi, barbecued pork, and garlic bread may seem like a strange Sabbath practice to many. But if you ask Gayle what helped us make it through one of the most challenging times in our marriage, she will tell you that was it. Each week, no matter how crazy it was at home, work, or school, we knew we had three hours of uninterrupted time with just each other. We called it our regular "Friday date night." But it was, in fact, a Sabbath practice. A chance to remember "who we are and whose we are" and why we are doing what we are doing.

That's what Sabbath practice is intended to be—relationship saving and life-giving.

The Discipline of Solitude

Sleep is a requirement of being human. While we can choose to delay or shorten our sleep, we cannot escape our need for it. Sooner or later, we fall asleep, whether we want to or not. It is the easiest of our "disciplines of finitude" to practice in that sense. However grudgingly, there's an inevitability to sleep that all human beings learn to accept.

In contrast, Sabbath is a voluntary discipline. While exhaustion can cause us to stop our work, we seem to be able to continue working for very long stretches without taking time off. Unlike the necessity of sleep, Sabbath has to be embraced intentionally.

So it is with our third discipline, solitude. In many ways, it seems even more optional than Sabbath. Most of us take time off during a given week. But if you are at all like me, weekends are as full of activity and people as your workweek. Solitude is simply hard to come by.

Why might that be?

One of the most helpful books I read in the last decade is Susan Cain's *Quiet: The Power of Introverts in a World That Can't Stop Talking*. The book helped me understand some things about myself, my family, and the world in which I live and work.

Cain argues that much of Western culture values extroversion over introversion and that those values are deeply embedded in our world of work. We value outgoing people who always speak up and are "on" all the time. We devalue people who are more reserved and reflective and who seem less "engaged."

Since there are about as many introverts as extroverts in the world, Cain's book persuasively argues that we marginalize a large segment of the population. To our detriment, we miss out on their significant contributions.

I realized that was true even in my immediate family. I'm more extroverted than my wife and both of my children. For much of my life, I thought of their introversion as a character flaw and tried to remake them into extroverts (like me!). Cain's book helped me appreciate their distinctive makeup. Even more, I came to see that I have something to learn from their introversion.

One of the great gifts my wife has given me is learning to desire solitude. Yearning for alone time came as naturally to her as breathing. She regularly needed—even craved—time for herself. I have to admit that for much of our life together, I misunderstood her instincts. Her desire for solitude came across as self-absorbed, but it was quite the opposite.

One of the characteristics of introverts is that they are more sensitive to external stimuli. Gayle has strong emotional empathy and picks up on emotional dynamics that I simply miss. That's a powerful gift, but it can also be overwhelming. Like information overload, emotional overload requires shutting off the flow. Hence, the need for solitude.

Solitude restores Gayle's capacity to empathize with others. Or, to say it differently, solitude restores her ability to be fully human with others without that capacity being distorted. Empathy can be distorted into emotional manipulation, anger, and even rage. Too much emotional connection can be exceptionally destructive, perhaps more so than not having enough empathy.

Solitude restores our sanity. Seemingly a paradox, withdrawal makes engagement possible. In a world where solitude is rare, is it surprising that so many relationships are profoundly distorted?

Learning to embrace the discipline of solitude enables us to use our power wisely.

For those who want to explore the practice of solitude further, I recommend Ruth Haley Barton's book *Invitation to Solitude and Silence: Experiencing God's Transformative Presence*. It is an accessible and practical guide on how to practice solitude in everyday life.

THE LIGHTED ROOM

A decade ago, I felt a need for time alone—for solitude. I was engaged in a challenging season at work. During the season of Lent, I took time every morning to sit in my study in silence. After my daily practice of praying the psalms, I tried to pay attention to the world around me and what was going on inside me. And I found myself writing stream-of-consciousness reflections in a journal.

One entry imaginatively captures for me the practice of solitude. I since have called it "The Lighted Room."* It reminds me of the space and time of my particular experience:

The darkness before the coming day. A room filled with light in anticipation of a light-filled day that requires no effort to illuminate.

An enclave of light. A protected place where we can truly be ourselves—although that too is harder than it should be. Why is being who we are so difficult? The temptation to be something and someone other than ourselves, shaped in the image of the One Who made us, is systemic in the world. "Don't let the world squeeze you into its own mold" [Rom. 12:2 Phillips].

How do we live faithfully, simply ourselves? What nourishes our core identity as image of God, beings not artificially distorted into a parody of ourselves?

The lighted room. The place to see ourselves as we were intended to be with no distortion. An accurate reflection of the Reflection.

Give us grace to see,
"Suffer us not to mock ourselves with falsehood
Teach us to care and not to care
Teach us to sit still
Even among these rocks."**

* Chi, *Life in the Intersection*, 9.
** T. S. Eliot, "Ash Wednesday," in *The Complete Poems and Plays, 1909–1950*, 67.

STEWARDING POWER WELL

Doesn't it seem odd that the practices that help us use power well negate its use? Sleep, Sabbath, and solitude are all acts of "not doing." As Jesus himself taught, denial of ourselves leads us to find ourselves (see, for example, Matt. 16:24–25).

The crucifixion is the ultimate expression of such self-denial. The all-powerful God of the universe submitting willingly to having all power stripped away. How could that be imaginable? Even more, how could that be true?

And yet it was. For Jesus, as for us, this is what it means to steward our power well. Jesus's death was not just a necessary price for humanity's failure and restoration. It was that, of course. But it was also the incomparable and ultimate demonstration of what God-like power looks like in its expression of self-restraint.

It is fitting to end these chapters on power as I began, with reference to Tolkien's *The Lord of the Rings*. In an encounter between the dwarf Gimli and the queen of the elves, Galadriel, Galadriel bestows the following blessing on Gimli: "I say to you, Gimli son of Gloin, that your hands shall flow with gold, and yet over you gold shall have no dominion."[12]

12. J. R. R. Tolkien, *The Lord of the Rings* (New York: Houghton Mifflin, 2004), 376.

That's a helpful image of God's intention for humanity's use of power. The challenge for human beings is using power without becoming enslaved by it. That's why the disciplines of finitude are essential in our lives. Their practice reminds us of our limits, thereby mitigating the seductive effects of power. They help us use power to serve others rather than dominate them.

As Jesus himself said: "The kings of the Gentiles lord it over them. . . . But not so with you; rather the greatest among you must become like the youngest, and the leader like one who serves" (Luke 22:25–26).

6

Wisdom and Leadership Formation

O ne year, our entire company visited the Pratt Fine Arts Center in Seattle for an evening of glassblowing. Each of us learned to form red-hot glass into art objects. We were astonished by a process that could turn otherwise brittle, unformed pieces of glass into something malleable that could then be shaped into stunningly beautiful works of art.

Leadership Formation through Suffering

Leadership formation is like that. Without the benefit of being "in the fire," we remain brittle and unformed. Becoming a wise leader comes at a price. As the sage of Proverbs says,

> Buy truth, and do not sell it;
>> buy wisdom, instruction, and understanding.
> (Prov. 23:23)

In an age where information is abundant and free, it may seem odd to say that truth and wisdom are expensive. But while information may be free, truth and wisdom are not. Wisdom requires personal investment and comes at a personal cost. As the wisdom

from above makes clear—especially as it is lived out in the life of
Jesus—that inevitably involves the fire of personal suffering.

But for that suffering to have a positive effect, we need our imagination shaped by stories that illustrate how such suffering works.
One particularly memorable narrative in the biblical tradition is the
story of Joseph, popularized by Andrew Lloyd Webber's musical *Joseph and the Amazing Technicolor Dreamcoat*.

If you are unfamiliar with the Joseph story, you can find it in
detail in the latter part of the book of Genesis (chaps. 37; 39–50). It
is well worth reading or reviewing before you read on.

The Joseph story is also summarized in Psalm 105:

> When he summoned famine against the land,
>   and broke every staff of bread,
> he had sent a man ahead of them,
>   Joseph, who was sold as a slave.
> His feet were hurt with fetters,
>   his neck was put in a collar of iron;
> until what he had said came to pass,
>   the word of the LORD kept testing him.
> The king sent and released him;
>   the ruler of the peoples set him free.
> He made him lord of his house,
>   and ruler of all his possessions,
> to instruct his officials at his pleasure,
>   and to teach his elders wisdom. (Ps. 105:16–22)

This retelling of the story highlights how suffering shaped Joseph as
a leader and will serve as the thematic framework for this chapter.

I like to think of leaders formed through suffering as "lead servants." That phrase is helpful because it places the emphasis on our
role as servants rather than as leaders. Even the popular phrase "servant leader" puts the grammatical if not the actual emphasis on being a leader rather than a servant. So, I've suggested reversing the

grammar to put the focus where it belongs. Further, the adjective "lead" suggests temporal priority rather than positional authority. In other words, a "lead servant" is someone who goes first, rather than someone who is merely in charge. As we will see, these themes are all underscored in the above psalm.

What in the World Is Going On?

How does the story of Joseph begin? The psalmist doesn't start with Joseph at all. Instead, the story is set in a much larger context. God "summoned famine against the land" (v. 16). Why would God do that? How would this evil turn into something good?

These questions remind us that there is much mystery in the world we are called to serve. But while much is mysterious, two things are clear from the start. First, as the text says explicitly, God is at work in the world for God's purposes. In other words, we are not at the mercy of merely impersonal or random forces. There is a purpose at work, even if it is opaque to us. Second, given the backdrop of the larger story, this God is always good. As I have noted before,

> The LORD is good to all;
> and his compassion is over all that he has made.
> (Ps. 145:9)

Despite what may appear to be contrary evidence, God is always working in the world for good.

The year before I launched my software business, the world came unglued for me. In the same week that President George H. W. Bush announced the beginning of the Persian Gulf air campaign, I was told that the company I was working for was being put up for sale or, absent a buyer, closed by the end of that year. It was hard to imagine a more difficult environment in which to hear the news, much less think about starting a new business. Having lived through the Arab oil embargo a couple of decades earlier, I knew the world had just become a much more dangerous place. Not just personally, but as a community and a nation, everything seemed at risk.

What might God be doing in such circumstances? Like firing up a furnace to create glass art, such events help shape those who find themselves in the middle of them. Leadership formation takes place not in a classroom but in the harsh realities of life. And that formation is deeply embedded in the particularities of our circumstances and is often as mysterious as God's work in the wider world. Still, God is at work in the individual and for the world. Joseph's story— one of the most extended and deeply moving narratives in the book of Genesis—gives us a look at the dynamics of that formation.

And paradoxically, the first insight about our formation from the story of Joseph is that leadership is not about us. Instead, it's about God's larger purpose in the world. And consequently, it's about our formation as leaders for the sake of the world. That's why we are called lead *servants*.

GOING FIRST WHERE NO ONE HAS GONE BEFORE . . .

Going first is often enviable. Who doesn't want to be the first to score tickets to an otherwise sold-out concert or sporting event? Who doesn't like to be the first to try the latest iPhone? Who wouldn't want to board an airplane first and find space for carry-on luggage? Being able to go first is usually a good thing. But then again, sometimes it's not. Who wants to be the first to take out the garbage, clean up a mess, or deal with an intractable problem at work?

It's the latter kind of going first that we find in the Joseph story. As the psalmist puts it,

> [God] had sent a man ahead of them,
> Joseph, who was sold as a slave. (Ps. 105:17)

As we saw previously, Joseph finds himself part of a global drama. And God is the prime mover with Joseph, as with the impending famine. Not only is God actively engaged in world-shaping events, but God is also involved in the lives of individuals, even when that engagement is unseen and perplexing.

The two verbs that inaugurate Joseph's leadership formation in Egypt are worth pondering. Joseph is both "sent" and "sold." Those two words don't usually go together. We are reminded that Joseph's sending is hidden in the act of being sold by his brothers into slavery in Egypt. That's a helpful insight when things go badly for us. It's easier to see our purpose when we flourish in our work. But what happens when we are sold out despite our best efforts?

That was one of my questions when my business was sold during the Persian Gulf War. Despite my best efforts, our corporate sponsors were divesting the business I had invested my life in. And conflicts arose within our team about the future of that business. One of our team members even brought in questionable investors in pursuit of a dubious business strategy. I have to admit that I felt sold out by others who were once close to me.

The Joseph story reminds and encourages us that God's providence is at work in our lives in the most challenging circumstances and—as we shall yet see—for the most unimaginable results. It's worth noting where Joseph winds up, having been sent and sold as a slave. Joseph dreamed of an exalted position of leadership where his parents and siblings would bow down before him. Instead, he finds himself in a dungeon in Egypt, abandoned by his family and those he had already served.

Extraordinarily, we discover that Jesus does willingly what Joseph does under compulsion. As the apostle Paul writes, Jesus,

> who, though he was in the form of God,
> did not regard equality with God
> as something to be exploited,
> but emptied himself,
> taking the form of a *slave*. (Phil. 2:5–7, emphasis added)

James and John, two of Jesus's inner leadership circle, also dreamed about fame and glory. Jesus's response is telling: "You do not know what you are asking. Are you able to drink the cup that

I drink, or be baptized with the baptism that I am baptized with?" (Mark 10:38). With a bravado that is all too common for those of us in leadership, they answered that they were able. Of course, they had no idea. Like Joseph early on, James and John imagined leadership as power, status, and privilege. They, like Joseph, will learn that God's model for leadership results, paradoxically, in becoming a slave.

And the greatest among them must go first.

FACING FUTILITY INSTEAD OF FRUITFULNESS

Some seasons of leadership are satisfying. Perhaps these seasons come after completing an important project, releasing a new product or service that delights our customers, or finishing a great team-building event. We know it when we experience it. At times like these, we feel blessed with work.

Of course, other seasons are precisely the opposite. We wonder if the project we work on matters, whether our new product or service will ever see the light of day, or whether we can ever get our team on the same page!

Not so long ago, I had lunch with a young business colleague who had an excellent job. Nevertheless, he struggled with a lack of meaning and purpose in his work. He believed that work should be an expression of God's calling in his life. Still, he couldn't reconcile that conviction with his lack of personal connection to his work. If God called him to his work, shouldn't he find meaning and purpose in that work? Why did he have a sense of futility about the work itself?

The story of Joseph reminds us that the answer to that question is complicated. Joseph's work begins by being betrayed by his brothers and sold into slavery in Egypt. Once there, Joseph distinguishes himself as a servant of Pharaoh's captain of the guard, Potiphar, who gives him broad responsibility for his household. But once again, he is betrayed, this time by Potiphar's wife. Having failed to seduce

Joseph, she accuses him of trying to seduce her. In a fury, Potiphar has Joseph locked up. As Psalm 105 notes,

> His feet were hurt with fetters,
>> his neck was put in a collar of iron. (v. 18)

Joseph had worked for Potiphar with distinction and devotion. Everything in Potiphar's household had flourished under Joseph's management. And in response to the illicit advances of Potiphar's wife, Joseph demonstrated impeccable personal integrity and loyalty to Potiphar.

Despite his competence and character, Joseph winds up in a dungeon in Egypt. Once more, Joseph winds up experiencing the antithesis of his dreams. For a second time, Joseph feared that his dreams and his work would be futile.

What am I doing here? Why does doing good lead to nothing but a dungeon? What's the point of faithfully working for others when it results in futility? It's easy to imagine Joseph wrestling with these questions as the years of imprisonment stretched on.

But, in the darkness of the dungeon, something happens to Joseph. The Book of Common Prayer helpfully translates the latter part of the verse as "iron entered into his soul."[1] That's a process that the apostle Paul would later describe this way: "suffering produces endurance, and endurance produces character, and character produces hope" (Rom. 5:3–4). Of course, not everyone who suffers responds in this way. It is possible to become bitter instead. Undoubtedly, Joseph had plenty of reasons and time to indulge in such a response. It would have been easy for such bitterness to have grown to full flower in Joseph. But it didn't.

Learning to suffer the futility of our dreams and endure in faith is not a popular leadership lesson. Joseph reminds us that it is a necessary one.

---

1. See "Psalm 105," The Church of England, accessed June 13, 2023, https://biblehub.com/commentaries/psalms/105-18.htm.

FORMATION IN THE LAND OF THE FORGOTTEN

Some of my friends say they are "in the pits" when things go badly. What they mean metaphorically Joseph experiences literally. Joseph finds himself in a pit in Egypt. He has been betrayed by his brothers, Potiphar's wife, and finally by Pharaoh's cupbearer, who forgot Joseph's kindness to him while in jail. It doesn't get much worse than this. Three times Joseph has been forgotten: by family, at work, and even after an act of intentional kindness.

Leadership formation is a long, painful process. We live in an age of abundant, easy-to-consume leadership advice. But learning about leadership is not the same as becoming a better leader. For one, knowledge and practice are two different things. For another, the challenge of becoming a good leader is not just a matter of personal commitment and effort. Instead, the story of Joseph reminds us that the formation of a leader's character through suffering, often over long periods, is essential.

During Joseph's long stretch of suffering, "the word of the LORD kept testing him" (Ps. 105:19). This image of being tested is of a precious metal being refined by fire (see, e.g., Ps. 12:6). Like refining silver, character formation requires not only extended time in a furnace but multiple repetitions.

I mentioned earlier the difficult season when my company was being sold. A decade followed where we had extraordinary success in working with our business colleagues at Herman Miller. Then I decided to take some time off to serve on nonprofit boards and to have more extended time with family. I had spent an inordinate amount of time and energy on my business during the prior decade, so it seemed an appropriate change of pace and focus.

I have to admit that I thought that time off would be a chance to enjoy the fruits of our labors. And there was some of that. But in God's providence, it also turned into a season of significant suffering for me and my immediate family. And that caught me by surprise.

As human beings, we have the freedom to choose how we respond in times of formational suffering. Learning to embrace the suffering we experience goes against the grain. Usually, I look for a quick way out. Nevertheless, the fire needs time to do its work. T. S. Eliot captures this remarkable dynamic in these words:

> Love is the unfamiliar Name
> Behind the hands that wove
> The intolerable shirt of flame
> Which human power cannot remove.[2]

"The intolerable shirt of flame / Which human power cannot remove" is what we are called to embrace in times of formational suffering. There's no way around it. Or, as some today might say: "the only way out is through." And each of us will face this in some form, perhaps many forms, in our journey of leadership formation. Like Joseph, we will experience times and places where we feel alone and forgotten: by family, by friends, at work, and, perhaps most cruel of all, after acts of deliberate kindness. We are formed, tested, and refined in the Land of the Forgotten.

The good news is that God does not forget us. As the prophet Isaiah said long ago,

> Can a woman forget her nursing child,
>   or show no compassion for the child of her womb?
> Even these may forget,
>   yet I will not forget you. (Isa. 49:15)

In the Land of the Forgotten, God remembers. And that will make all the difference for Joseph—and for us.

2. T. S. Eliot, "Little Gidding," in *The Complete Poems and Plays, 1909–1950* (New York: Harcourt Brace, 1980), 144.

DISCOVERING THE OUTER AND INNER FREEDOM TO SERVE

A young mom has trouble getting her preschool son to stay seated. After several skirmishes, she finally warns him, "Sit down, or I'll make you sit down!" Reluctantly, the child complies. After a few minutes, he turns to his mother and says, "I'm sitting down, but I'm still standing up on the inside!" It's a familiar compliant yet defiant moment for all of us who have raised strong-willed children. But it's also a helpful illustration of the difference between our inner and outer lives.

Imprisonment can be an experience of the heart as well as the body. Being set free physically is no guarantee of inner freedom. Joseph has been mistreated by family, at work, and despite his acts of deliberate kindness to others. He's been betrayed three times in over a decade and finds himself forgotten in a dungeon in Egypt. Still, the story reaches a turning point:

> The king sent and released him;
>   the ruler of the peoples set him free. (Ps. 105:20)

Joseph finds himself physically free. But will he experience corresponding interior freedom? Or will resentment and bitterness toward his betrayers and captors dominate his future?

No doubt, Joseph struggled with the memories of his imprisonments. He even named his firstborn son Manasseh, to, he said, "forget all my hardship and all my father's house" (Gen. 41:51). And those memories resurface during Joseph's encounter with his brothers later in the story. But the narrative ends with Joseph demonstrating generosity in forgiving his brothers. When confronted by his brothers' anxiety about what Joseph would do to them after the death of their father, Joseph reassures them with the seminal insight about suffering and leadership formation: "Even though you intended to do harm to me, God intended it for good, in order to preserve a numerous people, as he is doing today" (Gen. 50:20).

It is hard-won wisdom, paid with the price of Joseph's suffering. It wasn't easy for Joseph to learn and live this insight. I know it isn't easy for me. When we suffer unjust treatment while its perpetrators seem to flourish, it's easy to become discouraged or retaliate.

So, what sustains the inner freedom of heart, mind, and soul that enables us to become lead servants of others, even while suffering the consequences of their betrayals? What Joseph must have learned in his imprisonments the psalmist describes elsewhere in this way:

> Whom have I in heaven but you?
> And there is nothing on earth that I desire other
> than you.
> My flesh and my heart may fail,
> but God is the strength of my heart and my portion
> forever. (Ps. 73:25–26)

God alone can sustain the freedom in us to love even our closest enemies. Learning to love God alone enables us to love all others rightly.

Learning to Serve Well

After setting Joseph free, Pharaoh went one step further:

> He made him lord of his house,
> and ruler of all his possessions. (Ps. 105:21)

Joseph dreamed of such a day. The beloved and favored son of Jacob had visions of becoming a leader. And those dreams centered on his relationship with his family. He could not have imagined then what was now clear. He would lead the most powerful and advanced civilization of its day—the Egyptian Empire. In an astonishing reversal, Joseph transformed from a forgotten prisoner of Egypt to its prime minister. Pretty intoxicating stuff for a young man who had just turned thirty.

Coming into power at any age can be dangerous. Will we wield our newly found power well? The Joseph story illustrates and reinforces some insights that we've discussed before about how to resist power's corrosive aspects.

First, remember the purpose for which our power is given. Joseph's opportunity to lead Egypt comes for a reason: he is to save people from the coming famine. A healthy vision for leadership is centered on those served by the leader. And that vision is necessarily inclusive, not parochial. Note how Joseph's vision of his work expanded over time. Beginning with his extended family, his leadership horizon grew until it encompassed the known world. In the end, not only his family, not only his fellow Egyptians, but "all the world came to Joseph in Egypt to buy grain" (Gen. 41:57).

Developing an appropriately farsighted mission keeps us from making the nearsighted mistake of focusing on the necessary instruments of power for their own sake. Instead, we can wield them for the well-being of all those entrusted to our care.

Second, remember the essential virtue of humility. Joseph's interactions with Pharaoh during his rise to power are suggestive (see Gen. 41). "I have had a dream, and there is no one who can interpret it," said Pharaoh. "I have heard it said of you that when you hear a dream you can interpret it." Joseph replied, "It is not I; God will give Pharaoh a favorable answer" (Gen. 41:15–16). Rather than focusing on his gifts of wisdom and discernment, Joseph pointedly redirects Pharaoh's attention to God and God's concern for Pharaoh as the leader responsible for Egypt.

It's easy to forget or ignore God's work among those we serve. In another notable moment of humility, Joseph said about Pharaoh's dreams, "God has revealed to Pharaoh what he is about to do" (Gen. 41:25). Joseph could rightly have said that God revealed this to him and not to Pharaoh since the dreams were unintelligible to Pharaoh. Instead, he acknowledged God's giving the dreams to Pharaoh in the first place. Acknowledging God's work among those we serve helps keep the focus off us.

Finally, it's worth noting again that power is intended to be a gift, not a necessary evil. Joseph comes into his own, not only by Pharaoh's decree but in fulfillment of God's purpose in history. And Joseph isn't just an aberrant example of God's providence in human history. Instead, the story of Joseph is God's intention writ large for human beings. All human beings—male and female—are to exercise power for the world's good. Still, as Psalm 105 says about Joseph, we must be forged in suffering particular to our circumstances for that dominion to be exercised well.

Developing Bifocal Vision

I still remember the day in fourth grade when, suddenly, I couldn't see the blackboard anymore. After a visit to the optometrist, I learned that I was nearsighted. Thanks to his good work and a new pair of prescription glasses, I was able to see the blackboard again. I can't imagine how I would have functioned the rest of my life without being able to see at a distance. In the same way, being metaphorically farsighted is essential to leadership. Seeing what needs to be done is critical.

Farsightedness is a core gift of leadership. Joseph's ability to see and understand what others did not opens the doors for his work as the lead servant of Egypt. He sees the implications of Pharaoh's dreams—there will be seven years of plenty followed by seven years of famine. And he simultaneously sees what should be done—reserve 20 percent of the good years' harvests as a reserve to sustain the land during the famine.

Leadership requires both insight into the fundamental problems facing an organization and an understanding of the trajectory of their resolution. Further, leaders must mobilize their organizations to engage the needed work. That seems to be the meaning behind Joseph's instructing Pharaoh's "officials at his pleasure, and [teaching] his elders wisdom" (Ps. 105:22).

However, Joseph isn't just a good idea person. Sometimes we separate ideas from their implementation. In contrast, in ancient

Hebrew thought, wisdom holds the two together. As the sage in
Proverbs said about wisdom: "I am both Insight and the Virtue to
live it out" (Prov. 8:14 Message).

Similarly, modern business wisdom argues that strategy and execution should always be connected.[3] Joseph embodies the strategic
insight he was given: "And Joseph went out from the presence of
Pharaoh, and went through all the land of Egypt. . . . He gathered up
all the food of the seven years when there was plenty . . . and stored
up food in the cities; he stored up in every city the food from the
fields around it" (Gen. 41:46, 48).

Still, we might wonder how Joseph's wisdom was formed. A couple of narrative comments in the story of his imprisonment in Egypt
are significant. First, "The chief jailer committed to Joseph's care all
the prisoners who were in the prison, and whatever was done there,
he was the one who did it" (Gen. 39:22).

And when a couple of Pharaoh's senior staff were jailed, "The
captain of the guard charged Joseph with them, and he waited on
them" (Gen. 40:4).

While Joseph waits for his farsighted dreams to come to pass, he
pays close attention to serving those in front of him. Perhaps this
story provided Jesus with the narrative context for his famous aphorism: "Whoever is faithful in a very little is faithful also in much"
(Luke 16:10).

In that sense, those with leadership responsibilities must have
"bifocal vision," the ability to see what is immediately before them
as well as far into the distance.

That's particularly important for those of us who don't reach
the satisfying conclusion that Joseph experienced. As the recent
COVID-19 pandemic taught all of us, any of us can find ourselves
done before we are finished. Like Tolkien's character Niggle, whom

3. See, for example, Paul Leinwand and Joachim Rotering, "How to Excel
at Both Strategy and Execution," *Harvard Business Review*, November 17, 2017,
https://hbr.org/2017/11/how-to-excel-at-both-strategy-and-execution.

I mentioned in chapter 2. We need continual reminders to employ bifocal vision so that we can serve those entrusted to our care even as we struggle with our current experiences.

As the apostle Paul, who knew something of being formed in this life through suffering, said, "For this slight momentary affliction is preparing us for an eternal weight of glory beyond all measure" (2 Cor. 4:17). Whatever our circumstance in this life, that promise should encourage us to remain faithful in our present work, even as it makes us tingle with anticipation at what is yet to come.

7

Wisdom and Leadership Imagination

One of my favorite professional conferences in the 1980s was called SIGGRAPH. Every year, people gathered from all over the world to hear the latest research papers on computer graphics techniques and see the latest computer graphics hardware and software.

Tens of thousands of people met to see what was previously inconceivable. Many of the technologies that we now take for granted— 3-D virtual reality, feature-length animated movies, lifelike video games—had their origins at SIGGRAPH. No wonder it was always the highlight of my year.

In addition to showcasing the latest and greatest technology, the conference provided opportunities for professional education. One of the most unusual and memorable seminars I attended was called "Drawing the Natural Way." I was drawn to it (pardon the pun) because I always found art difficult. Ever since fourth grade, no matter how hard I tried, I couldn't manage anything better than a stick figure. And even those drawings were marginal. While I did well in most of my classes, art was a completely different story.

That SIGGRAPH seminar helped me understand why.

Our instructor began by having us draw a picture of a landscape. After a painful few minutes, I came up with my usual stick-figure sketch. She then turned the original picture upside down and asked us to draw it again. To my surprise, my resulting drawing looked much better. It looked less like stick figures and more like the actual picture. Most people sitting around me had similar experiences. And, of course, we all wondered why.

The instructor offered that modern education teaches us to think abstractly rather than concretely. We learn ways of looking at the world that help us develop generalizations (theories and models) rather than paying attention to the details, to see what is actually there. My stick-figure drawings were my brain's abstract way of expressing what I saw. A stick-figure person represents a real person. A stick-figure house is intellectual shorthand for the details of a real house.

By turning the picture upside down, my instructor forced me to pay closer attention. The upside-down picture was just different enough that my mind found it more challenging to "see" the abstraction rather than the reality. An upside-down person doesn't look quite like a normal person. An upside-down house doesn't look quite like a real house. So my mind had to pay closer attention to make sense of what it saw. In effect, I had to turn off rather than engage the abstracting part of my brain. And a drawing that reflects what is actually there was the result.

One of the things I learned that day was how my life had trained me to see the world abstractly. The capacity to abstract, to generalize, is without a doubt a great gift. Much of modern science and technology would be impossible without it. But it is only one aspect of the human mind. Another essential one is rooted in a different way of seeing.

WHY POETRY MATTERS

While being able to draw a picture accurately is a good thing, becoming a visual artist isn't a necessity for being a wise leader. At least for most of us. More critical is being able to see the world accurately and to imagine a different future. And then to communicate that vision compellingly so that others can internalize and act on it.

While good theories and solid analyses can contribute to that kind of seeing and communicating, they are not the principal means. More important is something that is rooted in a different part of our human capacity. Some call that additional capacity the poetic imagination.

Poetic imagination is a way of seeing and saying things differently. British poet Malcolm Guite puts it this way: "The poetic imagination ... [redresses] an imbalance in our vision of the world and ourselves ... [it] is a necessary complement to more rationalistic and analytical ways of knowing."[1]

When I teach on wise leadership, I sometimes ask my students to read Guite's book, *The Word in the Wilderness*. I have found the book helps students see the world differently. In his introduction, Guite begins by arguing that poetry changes the way we read: "Poetry asks to be savoured, it requires us to slow down, it carries echoes, hints at music, summons energies that we will miss if we are simply scanning. In this way poetry brings us back to older ways of reading and understanding both the Word and the World."[2]

I had a friend who was a voracious reader and who devoured books at a rate that made me marvel. And envy. Every time I heard of the latest books he had just finished, I could only sigh. I wished I could be like him. At one point, he confided in me that he had learned to speed-read at an early age. It was a valuable skill, particularly for going into academic life. The sheer volume of material he had to read to stay current beggared belief. Such was the reality of his professional life. And I understood and resonated with his struggle. I had my version of his problem as someone running a technology business. Keeping up with the steady torrent of technology developments and new business challenges was overwhelming for me too.

But despite the challenges of information overload, Guite reminds us that there are important and "older ways of reading and

---

1. Malcolm Guite, *The Word in the Wilderness* (London: Canterbury, 2014), ix.
2. Guite, *Word in the Wilderness*, x.

understanding," to which the poetic imagination calls us. Not everything can be speed-read. Not everything can be summarized in bullet form. Not everything can be found in an executive summary. Some things need soak time. Some require us to sit, listen, and pay attention—like poetry. As Guite aptly says, the ancient practice of *Lectio Divina*,[3] where we hear and reflect on the same passage of Scripture over and over, provides us with a helpful, countercultural example of hearing and seeing, which can be applied to more than just our spiritual disciplines.

It's worth noting that such a way of reading is not simply trying to figure out what a passage means. As a mathematics student, I remember reading a college text entitled *Abstract Algebra*. It was aptly named. It was so abstract that the arguments were very hard to follow. I remember one evening spending half an hour reading the same few sentences, over and over, trying to follow a vital piece of logic for an important mathematical argument. I had to read, reread, and think hard to make sense of it. Finally, I got it, and the argument made sense to me.

I felt like the punch line of a math joke, where two people are standing at a whiteboard looking at some equations. One person said that the result was obvious. The other said it wasn't. After twenty minutes of study, the second person finally said, "You're right. It *is* obvious." Yeah, right, but only in retrospect!

The poetic imagination isn't about the hard work of rationally figuring out what you are reading. The latter is a critical skill, but it uses a different part of our minds. The poetic imagination engages us in a way other than thinking hard about something, in the sense that we usually mean. But like hard analytical thinking, poetic imagination *does* require time and practice to cultivate. Most who have learned more analytical and abstract ways of thinking may find it a bit alien, but it can be learned.

I've used *The Word in the Wilderness* with my leadership students because it includes a set of daily reflections on particular poems.

3. Guite, *Word in the Wilderness*, x–xi.

Guite helps readers thoughtfully engage with the material to see how the poems work and what insights can be drawn from them. Like going with an expert guide on a tour to a foreign land, Guite helps readers understand what they are seeing, what the historical (and in this case, literary) connections are, and why that might be important to them. Both the book's form and content provide an excellent primer on how to read poetry and develop a poetic imagination.

Guite says that "as poetry begins to change the way we read, it also starts to influence the way we think and see."[4] That's essential to our task of leadership. As I noted above, one of the most basic tasks and challenges is to "define reality." And that means we need to develop our unique imaginative faculties to see the world as it is. And as it could be. Poetry helps shape our capacity to see and say things differently.

POETRY'S PRACTICAL BENEFITS FOR LEADERS

Recently, there has been increasing interest in how poetry and a poetic imagination might be of value to people in business. Even a distinguished journal of management such as the *Harvard Business Review* has published articles describing possible advantages. One piece of note is entitled "The Benefits of Poetry for Professionals" by John Coleman.[5] Coleman notes four key points, which I reflect on in detail below.

1.   Poetry helps us "wrestle with and simplify complexity."

The analytical mind deals with complexity by developing theories and models that capture a phenomenon's essence. Scientists use

4. Guite, *Word in the Wilderness*, xi.
5. John Coleman, "The Benefits of Poetry for Professionals," *Harvard Business Review*, November 27, 2012, https://hbr.org/2012/11/the-benefits-of-poetry-for-pro.

mathematical equations to describe a multitude of complex physical phenomena. Surprisingly, this seems to work for many aspects of ordinary life. Even more surprisingly, these methods seem to work not only at the human scale but also in the vastness of space and the minuteness of the atom. The behavior of stars, planets, molecules, and subatomic particles can be described in astonishingly compact mathematical ways. As I noted before, this ability to explain simply and elegantly how the physical universe works is one of the significant contributions of science.

The poetic imagination does something similar but in a radically different way. Poetry uses compact language to hold together disparate and even paradoxical things. It allows us to see connections and experience resonances between what, on the surface, seem unrelated and dissonant. Consequently, poetry helps us order and make sense of the complex and chaotic worlds we inhabit. In Coleman's words, it helps us "wrestle with and simplify complexity."

Whereas analytical thinking describes fixed, inanimate ideas, the poetic imagination describes fluid, living relationships. Rather than opposing and competing explanations for reality, both are essential to wisdom.

Sadly, our secular and scientific culture has stressed one way of seeing over the other. We have an overdeveloped analytical capacity that throws our leadership out of balance. Hence the need to develop a poetic imagination for wise leadership.

Perhaps a physical illustration would be helpful. I grew up playing tennis and a fan of an Australian tennis professional named Rod Laver. Laver dominated the sport in the 1960s, being ranked number one globally from 1964 to 1970. Laver played left-handed before the advent of the double-handed backhand. As a result, he developed an exceptionally muscular left arm. I remember seeing a photo of Laver where his left arm looked twice the size of his right. It was impressive—and bordered on the grotesque. In becoming the best in the world, Laver had developed one part of his body to the point where it distorted his appearance. At least that's how it seemed to me.

Of course, tennis has evolved since then. The two-handed back-hand changed the game, not to mention the resulting physique of tennis players. Players today have more physically balanced left and right sides. That's a helpful metaphor for our need for a poetic imag-ination. We need a better balance between developing an analytical mind-set and developing a poetic imagination as leaders.

Unsurprisingly, developing a poetic imagination takes time and energy. We need to learn to cultivate an appreciation for words that can help us communicate reality in more than abstract and analytical terms. Learning to use words to "define reality" takes work. And that means taking our use of language seriously—finding ways to say things that provide clarity and meaning to those who follow us. In the words of the poet T. S. Eliot, we need to find language

> Where every word is at home,
> Taking its place to support the others . . .
> An easy commerce of the old and the new . . .
> The complete consort dancing together.[6]

As a final note, Winston Churchill has been quoted as saying, "If you want me to speak for two minutes, it will take me three weeks of preparation. If you want me to speak for thirty minutes, it will take me a week to prepare. If you want me to speak for an hour, I am ready now."[7]

Churchill's witty if apocryphal saying reminds us that saying something important simply and memorably takes time. In my business experience, I spent more time analytically building finan-

6. T. S. Eliot, "Little Gidding," in *The Complete Poems and Plays, 1909–1950* (New York: Harcourt Brace, 1980), 144.

7. See AZ Quotes, accessed June 14, 2023, https://www.azquotes.com /quote/858888. The more likely source for a variation of the quote seems to be Woodrow Wilson. See Bartleby, accessed June 14, 2023, https://www.bartleby .com/73/1288.html.

cial models than imaginatively honing my words. That's a deficiency I hope this book helps correct.

2.   *Poetry helps us "develop a more acute sense of empathy."*

Abstract thinking focuses on impersonal realities, however vital they may be. The poetic imagination helps us remember that life is more than abstract, impersonal forces. Leadership, in particular, is about flesh-and-blood people. Connecting and communicating with them is integral to our leadership task. And essential to those things is developing empathy with others.

Poetry helps develop empathy because it requires us to "get inside" the poet's words. Poetic language carries layers of meaning that take time and effort to penetrate. It's rarely obvious what the poet is saying. That's one of the differences between prose and poetry. Almost by definition, poetry is not "prosaic."

As with my original story about learning to draw, one of the challenges for us as leaders is to pay careful attention to what is there and not assume we know ahead of time. Otherwise, we are at risk of mistaking stick figures for real people. As difficult and frustrating as it can be, we need to learn to get inside the heads and hearts of the people we serve and lead. That takes effort and time, much like learning to read poetry and to understand what the poet is trying to say.

In my experience with health-care leadership, one of the challenges modern workers face is cultivating empathy for the patient. At one level, that's surprising. Most people who become health-care professionals do so because they care about people. Helping people when they are ill and vulnerable motivates most men and women I know who serve the public in that way. But medicine is also a highly technical affair. And overlaid on top of that are expectations that the work is done efficiently and affordably. All that creates conflicting forces that can overshadow the importance of first connecting with and serving the patient.

A powerful video produced by the Cleveland Clinic illustrates what is easily forgotten or neglected. It is entitled *Empathy: The Human Connection to Patient Care*.[8] The video ends with the following question: "If you could stand in someone else's shoes. Hear what they hear. See what they see. Feel what they feel. Would you treat them differently?"

That's not just a challenge for health-care professionals. It is a challenge for all who aspire to be wise leaders. Do we hear what those we lead hear? Do we see what those we lead see? Do we feel what those we lead feel? Learning to pay attention to what is there is our way to answer these questions. And poetry can help us in developing those skills.

    3.   Poetry "develops creativity."

In one sense, poetry is disconnected from our everyday work. Poetry doesn't provide any direct guidance on what we should do today. Even worse, it's likely not even talking about anything related to our work. Its remoteness from the context and demands of our days makes poetry seem irrelevant to most people. But therein lies its genius.

Poetry allows us to switch mental contexts from our normal processes of problem solving. It's like visiting a foreign land with a different language and strange cultural practices. We learn to see and experience the world differently. Those different perspectives provide a fresh way of looking at our existing world when we return to our work.

When I started my business, I also sat on a local community hospital board. Given the demands of a start-up business, it would have been understandable for me to step back from board governance. But surprisingly, I found it helpful to think about the challenges of

---

8. See "Empathy: The Human Connection to Patient Care," YouTube, accessed June 14, 2023, https://www.youtube.com/watch?v=cDDWvj_q-08.

doing business in a very different industry. Switching mental contexts allowed me to take a break from focusing on my issues. While taking a break was mentally refreshing, it was also productive. Often in unexpected ways, I saw connections between health-care problems and those faced by my business, leading to new perspectives and solutions.

Poetry can do that, although in a more radical way. Not only does it change the content of our thinking, but poetry changes the very process by which we approach what we are thinking about.

Poetry helps us become more creative by teaching us to pay attention to the particular. As psychologist and researcher M. Csikszentmihalyi says, "The first step toward a more creative life is the cultivation of curiosity and interest, that is, the allocation of attention to things for their own sake."[9] As he notes, paying careful attention to what is right in front of us is the beginning of creative work, as is drawing imaginative connections between seemingly unrelated things. As modern neurobiology tells us, a part of our brain "lights up" that enhances memory and learning when we become curious.[10] That, too, is at the heart of and is the genius of what poetry offers.

When we read poetry, we are often puzzled by the use of words and the strangeness of the imagery. Some of my students complain that they find much of poetry incomprehensible. That can be disorienting and downright disturbing for many who are accomplished in their professions. They are not used to not understanding what they read. I try to reassure them that struggling to understand is pretty standard. Rather than throwing their hands up in despair, I counsel them to be curious. Why does the poet use this word? Where do

9. Mihaly Csikszentmihalyi, "Enhancing Personal Creativity," in *Creativity: Flow and the Psychology of Discovery and Invention* (New York: HarperCollins, 1996), 346.

10. Maanvi Singh, "Curiosity: It Helps Us Learn, but Why?" NPR, October 24, 2014, https://www.npr.org/sections/ed/2014/10/24/357811146/curiosity-it-may-have-killed-the-cat-but-it-helps-us-learn.

these images come from, and what might they mean? What other stories or poems might the writer be drawing from?

I tell my students that when I started reading T. S. Eliot's landmark poem *The Four Quartets* over fifteen years ago, I understood about 10 percent of the poem. But despite its opacity, I found it endlessly fascinating. In the intervening years, it's become part of my regular reading and reflection. In doing so, I learned to see the word and the world differently.

4.   Poetry *"infuses life with beauty and meaning."*

Poetry teaches us to look for the meaning in what we see. Poetry uses language and metaphor to address questions of meaning rather than questions of mechanics. Leadership is about helping people understand the meaning and significance of their work. People need to understand the "why" as well as the "what" and "how" of what they are doing.[11]

Ultimately, meaning brings us back to the question of the divine. Who is God? What is God like? How might God be working in the world? As I've suggested, wise leadership involves wrestling with such questions. Poetry provides language for us to explore those questions in ways complementary to rational argument.

Elizabeth Barrett Browning wrote a poem that illustrates poetry's expressive power:

> Earth's crammed with heaven
> And every common bush afire with God;
> But only he who sees, takes off his shoes.[12]

In three short verses, Browning demonstrates how poetic language contrasts with a more rational explanation for reality. Note

11. See, for example, Simon Sinek, *Start with Why: How Great Leaders Inspire Everyone to Take Action* (New York: Penguin Books, 2009).
12. Quoted in Guite, *Word in the Wilderness*, 23.

how her vivid language—"Earth's crammed with heaven / And every common bush afire with God"—compares with philosophical and theological descriptions of the world around us. These verses will be remembered long after such explanations have been forgotten. Poetry provides us with language that describes a compelling and memorable vision of reality.

And her verse compels us to action. "But only he who sees, takes off his shoes." Contemplation is one of the goals of poetry. But not mere reflection. Action is the ultimate intended outcome for the poetic imagination. But action requires someone who has vision, someone who sees. Otherwise, as Browning wisely noted, no one will want to take off their shoes.

In these short verses, Browning tells us something essential about reality. Equally important, she shows us how we can—through po-etry—engage that reality in a transformative way. And isn't that what wise leadership is about?

CONCEIVING THE INCONCEIVABLE

Like the creation story, what once was a "formless void" (Gen. 1:2) can be given shape and content in our minds and hearts. Our imag-ination springs to life, and something comes out of nothing. At its core, our imagination is the incubator of God's Spirit. In the language of one translation of the Genesis account, "God's Spirit brooded like a bird" over a "bottomless emptiness" (Gen. 1:2 Message).

Perhaps nothing is more human than our ability to imagine. That should not surprise us. We are made in the likeness of the One who loves to create things out of nothing. Our core identity as God's image-bearers resonates like a plucked string when we create some-thing new and original, something for the glory of God that serves the common good.

And there are many ways for us to express our imagination. My wife is an artist. Her works of watercolor delight and amaze me with their beauty. It's not hard to see her imagination at work, creating stunning paintings from a blank sheet of paper and an ordinary palette of paints.[13]

The role of the imagination isn't quite so evident in my work in business. Yet, whether it's designing a new product, developing sustainable strategies to build a business, or figuring out ways to organize a group of people to work well together, all these require imagination. In the myriad of human vocations, innumerable works large and small, multitudes of tasks mundane and extraordinary, imagination is the spark of life.

"How are you at bringing order out of chaos?" It's one of my favorite questions for people interviewing for a new job. For me, that's not just about a person's ability to deal positively with rapid change, although that's included. More importantly, it's a question of the quality of their imagination, their ability to envision and embody a constructive future, rather than succumbing to the inherently disruptive and often destructive forces of change. In leadership, the importance of being a nonanxious presence in times of upheaval is well established. It is part of how we bring order out of the chaos of disordering change. Still, what gives us the ability to sustain a nonanxious presence? I would suggest that our imagination roots us in chaotic times.

But there is another sense in which imagination is conceiving the inconceivable. In the way I've used the word so far, "conceiving" means the ability to envision. Yet another meaning for the word is the beginning of new life. In that sense, our imagination is a living receptacle by which we bring something new and alive into the world. That insight is helpful for at least two reasons.

First, our imagination is intended not merely to generate ideas but to result in life. Ultimately, the purpose of the human imagination is embodied formation, not disembodied information.

Second, the fruit of our imagination is not just the work of our own minds and hearts. It is the consequence of a relationship initi-

13. See, for example, Gayle Chi, *Fall Bounty*, 2015, at https://depree.org /wise-leader/image-9.

ated by God's Spirit, even when it goes unacknowledged by us and even if we are unaware of that work within us. The good gifts that result from our imagination come from outside of us:

> What no eye has seen, nor ear heard,
> nor the human heart conceived. (1 Cor. 2:9)

A vibrant imagination is not optional for those of us called into leadership. It is essential to the way we serve those who follow us. Of course, we express our imaginations differently, which is also God's gift. Nevertheless, as those who are to serve people by leading them into the future, we must participate in conceiving the inconceivable.

WHY PUZZLE PETER?

The story of the apostle Peter's encounter with the Roman centurion Cornelius serves as a turning point in the early Christian movement. What started as a mainly Jewish-focused message turned out to have much broader implications. The aftershocks of that encounter would raise questions that challenged the early church for much of the first century.

In reflecting on this story, I was struck by the difference between God's encounter with Cornelius and God's encounter with Peter. In the opening part of Acts 10, Cornelius has an angelic vision where he is told, directly and plainly, to send for Peter. Cornelius isn't told why he should send for Peter, and he isn't given any indication of what Peter might have to say. Nevertheless, the instructions are unambiguous.

Contrast Peter's experience. Peter sees the now-famous vision of a sheet being lowered from the sky, containing all sorts of animals. Along with the vision, Peter hears God's instruction to kill and eat. Being a faithful Jew, Peter responds, "By no means, Lord; for I have never eaten anything that is profane or unclean" (Acts 10:14). And this happens not once but three times.

Both men receive a vision from God. But Cornelius's vision is direct and actionable. Peter's is obscure and leaves him scratching his head. As Scripture puts it: "Peter was greatly puzzled about what to make of the vision that he had seen" (Acts 10:17). What could God mean by this strange vision? The Greek word translated "greatly puzzled" suggests someone trapped in their thinking with no rational way out.* And therein lies the clue. Peter needed a paradigm shift—a change in the way he saw the world—and not just another instruction on what to do in the immediate circumstance.

The dietary laws—what Jews were able to eat and not eat—were not only an essential religious practice for faithful Jews but served as identity markers for being Jewish. Along with keeping the Sabbath and circumcision, the dietary laws helped mark out who was a Jew and who was not. So, Peter's vision addresses more than just his dietary habits or even a specific act of obedience. Peter's vision challenges the very identity of who he was.**

When dealing with such deeply held convictions, rational explanations are rarely enough. We need to wrestle with our vision of reality. It seems to me that's what God is doing for Peter by communicating using such puzzling imagery. Metaphors and imagery can help penetrate mental defenses when rational arguments are fruitless.

I've lived most of my life in the Greater Seattle area. Seattle is well known as one of the most secular regions of the United States. Few people here are interested in conversations about religious matters, especially about the Christian tradition. But what I find interesting is that the visual and imaginative arts, including movies and novels, provide a way to talk about ultimate things that people can relate to. Philosophical and theological discussions seem to have limited appeal. Imagery and metaphor give access to truth that seems otherwise locked out by tightly held convictions.

Perhaps that's not unlike Peter's situation. Peter was in Jesus's innermost circle. And Peter likely heard Jesus say many times, "It is not what goes into the mouth that defiles a person, but it is what comes out of the mouth that defiles" (Matt. 15:11). But Peter was still a faithful Jew. And he knew that Jesus was too. Surely, Jesus couldn't have meant that the very markers of Jewish identity were going to be transcended by the gospel?

Peter needed help wrestling with a different vision of reality. And he needed help seeing it gradually. Rather than immediate clarity, seeing a dramatic but deeply puzzling vision helped Peter wrestle with a new reality. Truth necessarily engages our imaginative faculties. And that truth often appears ambiguous and paradoxical at first glance and requires time and reflection for us to understand.

Perhaps it is appropriate to let a poet have the last word on this reflection. Emily Dickinson wrote the poem "Tell All the Truth but Tell It Slant," which captures the slow but transformative effect of the poetic imagination. In it she says:

> Too bright for our infirm Delight
> The Truth's superb surprise ...
> The Truth must dazzle gradually
> Or every man be blind.***

WHY POETS MAKE GOOD BOARD MEMBERS

Luci Shaw is a distinguished American poet. I first met Luci when we joined the board of governors of Regent College in Vancouver, Canada. She was the "poet in residence" at Regent and had published extensively. I had never served on a board where someone like Luci was a member.

She proved to be a rare gift to the Regent board and a personal eye-opener for me. She had an exceptional ability to help the board see the whole rather than just the parts. Rather than just focusing on detailed issues, Luci regularly reminded us to look at the larger institutional situation. She also helped us to see and focus on the personal rather than just the programmatic and the strategic. She saw persons and relationships where many of us were merely thinking about financial results and programmatic growth. And she helped us to use our words wisely. She taught me how words could be used to obscure as well as to clarify. And she helped me to tell the difference.

Luci was a rare gift. I wish that every board I served on had someone like her. Perhaps a good place to start for those in governance leadership is to be aware of the need for that kind of person. Discussing whether poetic imagination (or something akin to it) should be on the list of essential skill sets would be a valuable conversation for any board-nominating committee.

* "Diaporeō," Bible Hub, accessed June 14, 2023, https://biblehub.com/greek /1280.htm.

** See N. T. Wright, *The New Testament and the People of God* (Minneapolis: Fortress, 1992), for a comprehensive treatment of this subject.

*** Emily Dickinson, "Tell All the Truth but Tell It Slant," in *The Poems of Emily Dickinson: Reading Edition* (Cambridge, MA: Belknap Press of Harvard University Press, 1998), https://www.poetryfoundation.org/poems/56824/tell-all-the-truth -but-tell-it-slant-1263. Accessed May 5, 2022.

8

WISDOM IN THREE DIMENSIONS

We pass through different stages in our physical development—as children, young people, and finally adults. While aspects of that progression can be found in our spiritual journey, seeing these physical stages as metaphors, not for spiritual advancement but as dimensions of our spiritual growth, is more helpful. In other words, we do not so much grow out of being childlike and youthful as we continually grow into those dimensions of being human.

In this chapter, I explore how wisdom is embodied in the dimensions of childlikeness, youthfulness, and maturity. It is easy to associate wisdom with maturity alone. But surprisingly, wisdom is often embodied in qualities associated not with age but with youth and even with infancy. At the same time, not everything related to being a child, a youth, or a person of old age is an expression of wisdom. We will take a look at each in turn.

THE WISDOM OF CHILDLIKENESS

In modern English, the words "childish" and "childlike" have entirely different meanings. "Childish" is a description that invariably has negative connotations. Adults behave childishly when they act impetuously or rudely, or throw temper tantrums.

In contrast, "childlike" has quite positive overtones. Adults be-

have in a childlike way when they display a sense of wonder or innocence about them.

Jesus himself picks up on the positive dimensions of being childlike. "At that time the disciples came to Jesus and asked, 'Who is
the greatest in the kingdom of heaven?' He called a child, whom he
put among them, and said, 'Truly I tell you, unless you change and
become like children, you will never enter the kingdom of heaven.
Whoever becomes humble like this child is the greatest in the kingdom of heaven'" (Matt. 18:1–4).

This saying of Jesus is helpful for our present discussion because
it highlights the positive quality of childlikeness. And Jesus describes
that quality not only as an entry requirement to the life of faith.
Unexpectedly, Jesus underscores the importance of childlikeness for
those who want to be "the greatest in the kingdom of heaven." In
stark contrast to the expectation that maturity would mean we would
grow out of being childlike, Jesus paints a picture of maturity that
has childlikeness as an integral element.

What might that look like?

To begin with, Jesus talks specifically about the state of children in
relation to the adults around them. Children are vulnerable and de-
pendent on the adults in their lives. Children cannot survive, much less
thrive, without the help and support of others. Children need to trust
others, even though that trust can sometimes be betrayed. The context
in which Jesus's words are spoken doesn't seem to point to childlike
wonder or innocence but to childlike vulnerability and trust.

In the middle of a very adult argument about power and being
powerful among Jesus's closest followers, Jesus calls a weak and vulnerable child into their midst to make his point. Being mature is not
about being powerful. Instead, cultivating childlike weakness is an
essential part of being the "greatest in the kingdom of heaven."

One of my favorite scenes from George Lucas's *Star Wars* anthology is when Luke Skywalker first meets Yoda.[1] Luke is expecting to
train with a master Jedi warrior. Instead, he finds a strangely decrepit

1. See *The Empire Strikes Back.*

creature that seems more like a playful child than someone who can help him learn how to become a Jedi knight. Luke says in frustration, "I don't even know what I'm doing here."

Jesus's vision of wisdom can be similarly disorienting. How did we wind up in such a strange place with someone who looks nothing like we imagined? Like Luke Skywalker, we often look for a powerful example to emulate, a "great warrior" leader. And, like Yoda, Jesus gently reminds us, "War does not make one great." As so often happens, our expectations are upside down.

For Jesus, childlike weakness and vulnerability are to be valued and cultivated. The more mature we get, the more critical they become. They are active reminders of our relationship with the Creator of all things. Paradoxically, the more we grow in faith, the more we become aware of our weaknesses and our vulnerability. If we are attentive, we become more and more conscious of how we are designed to trust in the God who sustains all of life and (again paradoxically) how our very brokenness as human beings imperils that relationship of trust. In both of those senses, we discover that God's faithfulness, not our own, sustains us in the journey.

Learning trust and vulnerability as we grow in maturity and wisdom is not easy.

Maturity can create the impression that we know what needs to be done and how to do it. We gain competence as we grow in wisdom, which is good. But competence can lead to an exercise of power disconnected from the living web of relationships, with God at the center. Competence and wisdom can create the illusion that we are sufficient in and of ourselves. That is why, as we discussed in the chapter on power, wise leaders need to learn that "vulnerability and dignity [are] not opposed to one another, and neither [are] dependence and dominion."[2]

Even for children, trust and vulnerability are learned traits. So for us, trust and vulnerability need to be developed as we grow in

2. Andy Crouch, *Playing God: Redeeming the Gift of Power* (Downers Grove, IL: InterVarsity Press, 2013), 102.

wisdom. While the fear of the Lord is the beginning of wisdom, it
is also its end.

As the ancient story of Abraham's sacrifice of Isaac illustrates, faith
is required at the pinnacle of our pilgrimage as well as at the beginning.
And as the Abraham story aptly demonstrates, there are plenty of twists
and turns (and failures!) along the way. We will fail to trust and be
vulnerable. Nevertheless, we are constantly called back to the posture
of childlikeness, like Abraham. In the greatest and final test of his faith,
Abraham's wisdom and maturity looked remarkably childlike. God
summons Abraham to offer up his one and only son, whom he loves. No
explanation. No promise that God will supply another alternative. Only
God's implicit "ask" that Abraham trust God, "like a little child."

Wisdom never outgrows the need to be childlike. Indeed, our
capacity to be childlike—like Abraham—needs a lifetime of cultivation. Learning to trust and be vulnerable is both the foundation
and culmination of our journey of wisdom. So is the delight and
wonder of childlikeness. Otherwise, we are at risk of missing what
G. K. Chesterton said in another context about God's own childlikeness: "It may be that He has the eternal appetite of infancy; for we
have sinned and grown old, and our Father is younger than we."[3]

PSALM 131

Psalm 131 encourages a lifelong journey of trust and vulnerability for those
who aspire to wise leadership. As leaders, we are vulnerable to developing
"high eyes" and a "lofty mind."*

[God], my mind has not been lofty,
my eyes have not looked high.
I haven't gone about with big ideas

3. G. K. Chesterton, *Orthodoxy*, quoted in Good Reads, accessed June 14,
2023, https://www.goodreads.com/quotes/19966-because-children-have
-abounding-vitality-because-they-are-in-spirit.

> or extraordinary deeds beyond me....
> Like someone nursed with its mother,
>   so my entire being is nursed with me.
> [Israel], wait for [God],
>   now and for evermore.**

As we grow in responsibility, we can begin to look down on others rather than continue to look up to God. That's one way to understand the psalmist's phrase of having high eyes. In our quest to be wise, we see others as being below us, not having achieved the level of insight, skill, or virtue that we have. And that's dangerous. The psalmist reminds us that our fundamental posture must always be to look up to God rather than down on others.

Similarly, growing in wisdom creates the opportunity for us to have responsibility for others. We start to manage teams of people rather than just ourselves. Pretty soon, we become responsible for whole organizations and institutions. We can become pleased with who we have become rather than remain focused on the concerns of others. And so, we develop a lofty mind about ourselves. And that too is dangerous. The psalmist reminds us that our fundamental posture must always be to hold a high opinion of others rather than of ourselves.

High eyes and a lofty mind can lead us to focus on "big ideas or extraordinary deeds" that are beyond our scope rather than on what we are called to do. We become preoccupied with saving the world, which is not in our job description but is in God's. This is particularly challenging today when the world's needs are paraded in front of our eyes by diverse media outlets. It's worth remembering that God values the small and hidden things we can do rather than the big and flashy things we can't. The psalmist reminds us that we are to do faithfully the little things we can, rather than trying to do the great things that God alone can.

Simultaneously, the psalmist reminds us that God provides all that is necessary for our identity and our work as wise leaders. Like a nursing mother, God satisfies our needs, allowing us to be who we are and do what we need to do. Our trust and vulnerability enable us to rest in God's care and provision like a nursing child. We have everything we need for who we are called to be and what we are called to do. Like a nursing child, we can consciously and intentionally exercise trust and vulnerability toward God, who provides all we need.

Finally, the psalmist encourages us to do that always and forever. Trust and vulnerability are not postures only for the beginning of our journey. They are our end as well as our beginning. Our hope should always be in God and not in ourselves.

* John Goldingay, *Psalms*, vol. 3, *Psalms 90–150* (Grand Rapids: Baker Academic, 2008), 533–39.

** John Goldingay, *The First Testament: A New Translation* (Downers Grove, IL: IVP Academic, 2018), 596.

THE WISDOM OF YOUTHFULNESS

Osmar Schindler's *David and Goliath*[4] captures young David's curious confrontation with Goliath and the Philistine army at the decisive moment.[5] In that painting, Goliath laughs uproariously at the incredible sight of a Hebrew youth approaching the battle-hardened Philistine army with a slingshot. Rejecting the serious instruments of warfare offered to him by King Saul, David comes to the battle with an almost surreal youthful *curiosity* and *playfulness*, as the run-up to the critical moment demonstrates.

"Who is this uncircumcised Philistine that he should defy the armies of the living God?" David had earlier asked the Israelite army. His oldest brother, Eliab—older but not wiser—takes this as David egging him and his countrymen into battle so that David could enjoy the show. "I know your presumption and the evil of your heart," he fires back at David. "For you have come down just to see the battle." But David responds not with the fear and anxiety of his elder brother but with the curiosity and playfulness of youth: "What have I done now? It was only a question" (1 Sam. 17:17–30).

Eliab, King Saul, and the whole Israelite army were struggling

4. Osmar Schindler, *David und Goliath*, 1888, available at https://depree .org/wise-leader/image-10.

5. The story of David and Goliath is recorded in 1 Sam. 17.

with the realities of the battle with Goliath and the Philistine army. It seems likely that the Philistines were champions of their ancient regional arms race. Goliath's sword was likely a technological marvel of the Bronze Age. As David would say later, "There is none like it" (1 Sam. 21:9). And Goliath himself was a marvel of genetic superiority. He was a giant of a man and a warrior without equal (1 Sam 17:4–7). It was enough to make battle-hardened men fearful and anxious. And rightfully so. Israel was faced with a technologically and biologically superior foe.

Sometimes, there seems to be no mature, rational way out. Even resorting to childlike trust—becoming like a nursing child as Psalm 131 counsels—is not enough. Action is necessary. But what kind of action is called for?

I would suggest that David gives us a glimpse of youthfulness as a dimension of wisdom. Whereas childlike trust can lead to passivity and mature reflection to rational dead ends, youthful creativity and playfulness offer us a "third way" to become wise leaders.

The biblical vision of wisdom has the essential qualities of creativity, curiosity, and playfulness embedded in its very essence. In a key passage of Proverbs, wisdom is personified as being present in the very work of creation. In describing wisdom and its work, the writer says:

> I was beside him as a craftsman.
> I was playing daily,
> laughing before him all the time.
> Laughing with the inhabitants of his earth
> and playing with the human race.[6]

In our serious work of becoming wise leaders, it is worth remembering that God's wisdom has a delightfully playful quality. In our fallenness, we seek to grow out of our childlikeness and youthful-

6. Prov. 8:30–31, trans. Tremper Longman III, *Proverbs* (Grand Rapids: Baker Academic, 2006), 203.

ness. What Chesterton said about becoming childlike is equally valid about being youthful: "We have sinned and grown old. And our Father is younger than we."

A dimension of youthful curiosity and playfulness characterizes the wise leaders I have known. A great example is my friend Bix Norman, formerly an executive at Herman Miller. Bix is a remarkably astute businessperson. He built a small Herman Miller subsidiary that focused on recycled office furniture into a game-changing business that served small to medium-sized office furniture customers. My company was fortunate to be Bix's technology partner in developing one of the critical pieces of his business strategy.[7]

What struck me about Bix's leadership was his ability to foster innovation and harness it for creative business ends. In that way, Bix was exemplary of Herman Miller's long tradition of creating unique and groundbreaking commercial office furniture, such as the Aeron Chair. But that tradition was not a guarantee of business success, even in a company with a storied history like Herman Miller.

My first meetings with Bix and one of his Herman Miller executive colleagues are a case in point. In my introduction to Herman Miller, I met separately with Bix and with one of Bix's colleagues. Bix's colleague assembled a large group—around thirty people or so, as I remember—and we had a long discussion about Herman Miller's needs and my company's technological capabilities. It was a thoughtful and serious conversation, but it lacked focus and clarity.

My conversation with Bix and his team was entirely different. Bix had a clear vision of what was important to him. He and his team were actively curious about what we brought to the table, and were willing to experiment with us in creating the software that their business needed. As we got to know them, I was struck by the sense of delight and joy in Bix's organization. There was a conscious focus on creating a playful and curious culture. But it wasn't play for its own sake.

A decade before I met Bix, I visited Xerox PARC (Palo Alto Re-

---

7. See Sandra J. Sucher, *Herman Miller (A): Innovation by Design*, Business Case Study (Boston: Harvard Business School, 2002).

search Center), which was renowned for developing leading-edge easy-to-use computer technology. PARC invented much of what would later find commercial success through Apple and other companies. Years before Apple's Macintosh, PARC had developed similar technologies.

PARC also had a remarkable culture of curiosity and playfulness. But the difference between PARC and Bix Norman's organization was that PARC's youthful curiosity and playfulness were not connected to the company's business strategy. There was no integral link between their culture of curiosity and playfulness and Xerox's product offerings.

For this discussion on leadership, the larger insight for me is that curiosity and playfulness must be an ongoing, integral dimension of human wisdom, not merely an interesting diversion. We need youthful curiosity and playfulness, but we need it integrated with childlike trust and vulnerability, and, as we shall see shortly, with mature discernment and courage.

For now, it is good to be reminded that wisdom and maturity need a certain kind of youthfulness. As the poet T. S. Eliot wisely observes, "Old men ought to be explorers."[8]

Youthful curiosity and playfulness help us avoid getting stuck, either by being unnecessarily passive or by finding ourselves at a rational dead end.

ON HUMOR AND HYPERBOLE

For those of us who are serious about wisdom, it's easy to go light on humor and hyperbole. That's particularly true for those from a Christian tradition that takes God seriously. Indeed, our relationship with the Creator of all things is a serious matter. Does God even have a sense of humor? Even more

---

8. T. S. Eliot, "East Coker," in *The Complete Poems and Plays, 1909–1950* (New York: Harcourt Brace, 1980), 129.

so with hyperbole. Exaggeration and truth seem like opposites. Would God ever exaggerate to make a point?

I recently read a book that I've had on my bookshelf for a long time. The book was written half a century ago by the respected Christian philosopher Elton Trueblood. The title of the book is *The Humor of Christ*.

Like Trueblood, I have to admit that most of my experience of the Christian tradition does not place a high value on Jesus having a sense of humor. Most Christian iconography shows Jesus with a serious, if not dour, facial expression. Notable by its exception is the picture called the "Laughing Jesus," created by Willis Wheatley.*

In the book's introduction, Trueblood tells of reading to his four-year-old son the passage in which Jesus says we should not try to take a speck out of our neighbor's eye when we have a beam in our own. Trueblood's young son began to laugh. It struck him as ridiculous that someone should have a beam in their eye, and even if they did, that they would then worry about their neighbor having a speck in theirs! What made him laugh should make us laugh. And it should remind us that Jesus had a sense of humor.

Trueblood argues that some of Jesus's teaching is unintelligible without appreciating his sense of humor. Take, for example, Jesus's stories about camels. Jesus said, "It is easier for a camel to go through the eye of a needle than for someone who is rich to enter the kingdom of God" (Mark 10:25).

Biblical scholars have long debated what Jesus meant by this saying. Was Jesus talking about a gate in Jerusalem called the "Eye of the Needle," which was so narrow that a camel could pass through only if its entire load was removed? Perhaps it's a metaphor for rich people having to divest themselves of their riches before they could enter God's kingdom.

But what if Jesus said this with a twinkle in his eye? What if it was deliberately hyperbolic and told precisely because its outrageousness made it memorable? If you doubt Jesus's intention in that story, it seems crystal clear in another story about camels. When critiquing the religious practices of the Pharisees, Jesus said that they strain out a gnat but swallow a camel (Matt. 23:23–24). No literal interpretation is possible. Jesus meant for the preposterous image to lodge in his hearers' imagination and memory. As indeed it has through the last two millennia.

Trueblood argues, "Of all the mistakes which we make in regard to the humor of Christ, perhaps the worst mistake is our failure, or our unwillingness, to recognize that Christ used deliberately preposterous statements to get His point across. When we take a deliberately preposterous statement and, from a false sense of piety, try to force some literal truth out of it, the result is often grotesque. The playful, when interpreted with humorless seriousness, becomes merely ridiculous."**

Jesus had a remarkable capacity to tell compelling and memorable stories. And that capacity is rooted in his playful use of hyperbole and humor. Without such a perspective, Jesus's teachings can quickly become distorted and made (to use Trueblood's vivid word) "grotesque." None more so than Jesus's sayings about what to do in response to sexual temptation.

Jesus taught, "If your right eye causes you to sin, tear it out and throw it away; it is better for you to lose one of your members than for your whole body to be thrown into hell" (Matt. 5:29). When I was at university, I read a story in the student newspaper about a fellow student who did precisely that, troubled by his struggle with sexual temptation. It was a tragic incident that reminds us of the consequences of misunderstanding humor and hyperbole.

Jesus's audience surely knew he was being hyperbolic and even humorous. After all, how can only your right eye cause you to sin? Do we sin with one eye closed?! Jesus's story is preposterous and ludicrous on its face. And that is the point. Jesus meant for the story to capture the imagination and stick with people. As Trueblood says, "There is good reason to suppose that Christ *meant* His words to sound preposterous. We spoil the figure, and lose all the robustness, when we tone it down."***

Jesus used humor to teach, not to entertain. There's no evidence that Jesus used humor merely to warm up an audience. Instead, Jesus used humor as a means to help his followers come to terms with who they are and what they are to do. "We seek humor for humor's sake. There seems to be little or none of this in the recorded words of Christ, where the purpose is always the revelation of some facet of truth which would not otherwise be revealed. The humor of Christ is employed, it would appear, only because it is a means to calling attention to what would, without it, remain hidden or unappreciated. . . . Humor is redemptive when it leads to comic self-discovery."****

Jesus's use of humor and hyperbole reminds us that curiosity (what in the world did he mean by that?) and playfulness (wasn't that funny and to the point!) are essential dimensions of wisdom. As Jesus demonstrates, having a good sense of humor is necessary for becoming a wise leader.

* See Douglas Todd, "Meet the Creator of the 'Laughing Jesus' (Photo)," *Vancouver (BC) Sun*, January 19, 2014, https://vancouversun.com/news/staff-blogs/meet-the-creator-of-the-laughing-jesus-photo.

** Elton Trueblood, *The Humor of Christ* (New York: Harper & Row, 1964), 46–47.

*** Trueblood, *The Humor of Christ*, 48.

**** Trueblood, *The Humor of Christ*, 52, 54.

THE WISDOM OF MATURITY

At last, we come to the dimension most commonly associated with wisdom: maturity. In Gaspar de Crayer's painting *The Judgement of Solomon*,[9] Israel's King Solomon renders his memorable judgment to divide the baby.[10]

In that case, two women brought before Solomon a baby whom each claimed to be her own. There were no witnesses that could distinguish between the women's contradictory claims. Solomon decided the case by offering to cut the child in two and give half to each. In horror, the natural mother offers to give the living child to the other woman. In contrast, the other woman, whose child had already died, would rather see the woman's son dead than give him up to his birth mother. Solomon discerned who the birth mother was in their responses and gave the child to her. It was a stunning outcome to a seemingly irreconcilable set of claims. No wonder that "All Israel

9. Gaspar de Crayer, *The Judgement of Solomon*, 1620–1622, available at https://depree.org/wise-leader/image-11.

10. See the story in 1 Kings 3:16–28.

heard of the judgment that the king had rendered; and they stood in awe of the king, because they perceived that the wisdom of God was in him, to execute justice" (1 Kings 3:28).

Solomon through this story demonstrates that wisdom requires mature *discernment* and *courage*. Discernment requires insight into human affairs. Solomon judged correctly that a birth mother would not want her child harmed, even if that meant she had to give the child up to another. And he judged correctly that the woman who was making a false claim to motherhood would have nothing to lose in her grief and jealousy. Consequently, he devised a shrewd test to see who the birth mother was.

But those general insights about human nature were not certainties. As we are all too aware in our day—and as I suspect Solomon was in his—there are mothers whose pathologies might overshadow concern for their own child. It was a risky and courageous move to put his discernment to the life-and-death test he proposed.

Wisdom requires discernment and the willingness to be courageous in the face of risk. Real-life discernment, particularly in important matters, rarely comes with certainty. While we may be confident, we are not sure. And that's why courage is so necessary. As we have argued before, the fear of the Lord—our faith in God and not our certainty in our rightness, even in our discernment—is the beginning and the end of wisdom.

Maturity and age are not the same thing. The painting shows a relatively young Solomon making this landmark judgment. That is consistent with where that story is told in the narrative of Solomon's reign. After all, it is the first story following Solomon's ascension as king and his prayer for wisdom to distinguish his rule (see 1 Kings 2:13–3:15).

In the same way, discernment and courage (maturity in the sense I'm using that word) can be found in young people and absent in those who are old. Or, to say it slightly differently, maturity is a dimension of wisdom that needs cultivation throughout our journey as wise leaders.

Why are discernment and courage so necessary?

For one, as I said before, the world in which we operate is neither morally neutral nor entirely good. There are plenty of actors who behave badly. As Jesus himself counseled in commissioning his leadership team, "I am sending you out like sheep among wolves. Therefore be as shrewd as snakes and as innocent as doves" (Matt. 10:16 NIV).

We must be neither naive nor simpleminded, and we must not be timid or cowardly. Instead, we must grow in our capacity for discernment and courage.

I am optimistic by nature. Some people tell me that's what it takes to be an entrepreneur. As a result, I find it easy to look for the best in people and circumstances. When the glass is half full, it often looks 80 percent full to me. I tend to downplay the negative—in both circumstances and people—and focus on the positive. While that can sound like an asset, it can lead to living in denial about the reality of the situation. I find Jesus's commissioning instruction and warning a helpful corrective. Jesus is a realist, not an optimist or, for that matter, a pessimist.

Thankfully, as I've mentioned before, I've had partners in business and in life that complemented my sometimes unfounded optimism. Both my wife and my business partners were much more critical in their assessment of reality. But their perspectives were not easy for me to hear. That was true, whether it was about the realities of parenting teenagers or adult children or the realities of our dealing with recalcitrant competitors or difficult employees.

To me, it is easy to confuse love with optimism. And that can lead to a lack of discernment and the associated courage to deal with what is actually there. As Steve Garber has asked insightfully, *"Can you know the world and still love it?"*[11] Facing the world as it really is, is the first task of love. Jesus knew that better than anyone. He understood and was willing to pay the ultimate price to make the world

---

11. Steven Garber, *Visions of Vocation* (Downers Grove, IL: InterVarsity Press, 2014), 22.

right again. As wise leaders, we need the requisite characteristics of discernment and courage to love the world as Jesus did.

Another reason discernment and courage are so necessary is that, in some conservative religious traditions, more emphasis is placed on childlike trust than on mature reflection and thought. Reflection and discernment are viewed with suspicion and even disdain. Personal spiritual experiences and "hearing God speak to me" trump the hard work of wrestling with what Scripture says and what implications it might have for us today. As someone once said, it feels like we have to check our brains at the door.

But that is contrary to what Jesus warns about in his commissioning words and contrary to what the apostle Paul says in his letter to the church in Corinth. There are similarities between the segment of the church that prizes personal spiritual experiences and the first-century church in Corinth. The latter had a similar preoccupation with revelatory gifts and experiences and downplayed the importance of rational thinking. In the middle of that context, Paul said, "Brothers and sisters, do not be children in your thinking; rather, be infants in evil, but in thinking be adults" (1 Cor. 14:20).

As Paul argues, it is a virtue to be innocent of evil but not to be naive in our thinking. Jesus said much the same. We need to do the hard and courageous work of wrestling with and discerning what the right thing is to do in our present historical context. Each generation is faced with doing that work in its day. And that requires the engagement of the totality of our human faculties—all our heart, soul, mind, and strength—to do well.

In particular, that requires our minds, our thinking. Undoubtedly, that requires the "renewing of [our] minds" (Rom. 12:2), as the apostle Paul knew from personal experience. After all, his own mind and life had been radically transformed by his encounter with the risen Lord Jesus Christ and the subsequent reworking of his understanding of who God is and what God is doing in the world.

In the same way, our journey to mature wisdom can be upended.

Discernment is not just a matter of applying a fixed grid to our way of seeing the world, no matter how right and wise we think that grid may be. Discernment requires the openness to change the way we see the world and our ability to make the right judgments about the world we see. In that sense, wise discernment is like a pair of glasses by which we can see the world differently, but which itself may require lens replacements along the way.

Cultivating Multidimensional Wisdom

We are three-dimensional beings after all. When we flatten that dimensionality—as in a photograph—something important is lost. We've all seen cardboard cutout pictures of people. No matter how realistic the photo is, it's easy to distinguish the person from the facade. So it is with real wisdom.

Fully dimensional wisdom—truly human wisdom—requires childlike *trust and vulnerability*, youthful *curiosity and playfulness*, and mature *discernment and courage*. These three dimensions of wisdom are hard to embody in an integrated way. It is easy to focus on one or even two dimensions and neglect the others.

One or two dimensions alone result in a distortion—a caricature—of wisdom.

Childlikeness alone can result in naive and simpleminded leadership. It can be susceptible to inappropriate passivity. Much like Jesus's description of "sheep among wolves," childlikeness alone subjects leaders to deliberately malign forces that wreak havoc among their followers.

Youthfulness alone can express itself in leadership that is undisciplined and unfocused. It quickly gives way to pursuing every plausible idea that comes along. It can waste precious resources in the name of creative exploration. It can also lead to an unfettered optimism about a future that never comes.

Maturity alone can express itself in leadership that is rigid and misguided. Habits of leadership can lose their vital connection with the present and become enamored (or is it armored?) with a real or imagined past. It can get trapped in ways of thinking that exclude unimagined possibilities. It can become overconfident in its ability to see and judge the world accurately and rightly.

So, how do we hold these three dimensions in tension and together?

My experience is that personal and circumstantial triggers push us into one dimension over another. Our fears and anxieties drive us to our comfort zone responses. As I mentioned earlier, my natural optimism can respond to challenging situations with childlike trust that things will work out. In my case, that can be a spiritual smokescreen that obscures my unwillingness to deal with the difficulties I'm facing.

Having all three dimensions before me helps me look at the situation I'm facing through three different lenses. Am I seeing the world accurately, and am I responding faithfully as I look at the problem from each dimension's point of view? These are helpful questions when I am inclined to respond to situations in a seemingly prewired way.

Epilogue

The very notion of wisdom implies that there are wise and unwise ways of being human. Most wisdom traditions suggest that not all ways of life are equal. And we know this to be true from personal experience. There are wise ways, and there are foolish ways of being human.

My search for wisdom, which began at an early age, has led me to a Christian vision of what it means to be human. That vision shares many commonalities with other religious and philosophical traditions about living wisely. My experience of the wisdom of my Chinese grandfather, which I shared in the introduction to this book, is but one personal example of that commonality.

But there is something distinctive about a Christian vision of wisdom, particularly as it applies to those of us in leadership. *Unlike wisdom that is ultimately about the impersonal use of knowledge and power over others, a Christian vision invites us into a wisdom that is personal and mutual to the core.*

It requires a willingness to engage in the particular circumstances of our lives, as part of a diverse community of persons, and a willingness to put everything we have and know at risk. It sees the use of power in the service of others and not itself. And it considers humility, trust, and vulnerability—what some might regard as weaknesses—as indispensable elements of wisdom and strength.

Finally, it is willing to not just think rationally but imaginatively about life. And not just to think about life but to be shaped and formed by it in the furnace of our sufferings.

The way of wisdom is neither simple nor easy. It requires our whole selves as human beings in its pursuit. But as the sage of the book of Proverbs puts it,

> [Wisdom] is a tree of life to those who lay hold of her;
> those who hold her fast are called happy. (Prov. 3:18)

And that wisdom is meant to be experienced and shared with those around us.

When Moses gave his last address to the people of Israel, just before they entered the land of promise, he described the result of the pursuit of that kind of wisdom. When Israel lives by God's teaching about what it means to be human, there will be those who see their lives who will say, "Surely this great nation is a wise and discerning people!" (Deut. 4:6).

In other words, people around us can recognize instinctively when they see wise leadership.

The world continues to wait and watch for people who could be described in that way. I hope this book makes a small contribution to the development of such leaders.

WORKS CITED

Alter, Robert. *The Hebrew Bible*. Vol. 1. New York: Norton, 2019.

Asimov, Isaac. *Foundation*. New York: Octopus Books, 1984.

Augustine. *Letters (83–130)*. Edited by Roy Joseph Deferrari. Translated by Wilfrid Parsons. The Fathers of the Church, vol. 18. Washington, DC: Catholic University of America Press, 1953.

Barton, Ruth Haley. *Invitation to Solitude and Silence: Experiencing God's Transformative Presence*. Downers Grove, IL: InterVarsity Press, 2010.

Bethge, Eberhard. *Dietrich Bonhoeffer: A Biography*. Revised and edited by Victoria J. Barnett. Minneapolis: Fortress, 2000.

Brueggemann, Walter. *Sabbath as Resistance*. Louisville: Westminster John Knox, 2014.

Buechner, Frederick. *Godric*. New York: HarperCollins, 1983.

Cain, Susan. *Quiet: The Power of Introverts in a World That Can't Stop Talking*. New York: Crown, 2012.

Canlis, Julie. "Self-Care Only Works in God's Care." *Christianity Today*, March 10, 2022. https://www.christianitytoday.com/ct/2022/march-web-only/lent-self-care-discipline-discipleship-works-gods-care.html.

Chesterton, G. K. *Orthodoxy*. Quoted in Good Reads, accessed June 14, 2023, https://www.goodreads.com/quotes/19966-because-children-have-abounding-vitality-because-they-are-in-spirit.

Chi, Uli. *Life in the Intersection*. Seattle: Self-published, 2011.

Coleman, John. "The Benefits of Poetry for Professionals." *Harvard Business Review*, November 27, 2012. https://hbr.org/2012/11/the -benefits-of-poetry-for-pro.

Collins, James C. "Level 5 Leadership: The Triumph of Humility and Fierce Resolve." *Harvard Business Review* 79, no. 1 (2005): 66.

Collinson, David. "Prozac Leadership and the Limits of Positive Thinking." *Sage Journals: Leadership* 8, no. 2 (2012): 87–107.

Crouch, Andy. *Playing God: Redeeming the Gift of Power*. Downers Grove, IL: InterVarsity Press, 2013.

Csikszentmihalyi, Mihaly. "Enhancing Personal Creativity." In *Creativity: Flow and the Psychology of Discovery and Invention*, 343–72. New York: HarperCollins, 1996.

De Pree, Max. *Leadership Is an Art*. New York: Currency Doubleday, 2004.

———. *Leadership Jazz*. New York: Doubleday, 2008.

Dickson, John. *Humilitas: A Lost Key to Life, Love, and Leadership*. Grand Rapids: Zondervan, 2009.

Dyrness, William A. *The Facts on the Ground: A Wisdom Theology of Culture*. Eugene, OR: Wipf & Stock, 2022.

Eliot, T. S. *The Complete Poems and Plays, 1909–1950*. New York: Harcourt Brace, 1980.

Francis, Pope. *Encylical on Climate Change & Inequality: On Care for Our Common Home*. Brooklyn, NY: Melville House, 2015.

Garber, Steven. *The Seamless Life: A Tapestry of Love and Learning, Worship and Work*. Downers Grove, IL: InterVarsity Press, 2020.

———. *Visions of Vocation*. Downers Grove, IL: InterVarsity Press, 2014.

Goldingay, John. *Exodus & Leviticus for Everyone*. Louisville: Westminster John Knox, 2010.

———. *The First Testament: A New Translation*. Downers Grove, IL: IVP Academic, 2018.

———. *Psalms*. Vol. 3, *Psalms 90–150*. Grand Rapids: Baker Academic, 2008.

Guite, Malcolm. *The Word in the Wilderness*. London: Canterbury, 2014.

Jones, Robert P. *White Too Long*. New York: Simon & Schuster, 2020.

Leinwand, Paul, and Joachim Rotering. "How to Excel at Both Strategy and Execution." *Harvard Business Review*, November 17, 2017. https://hbr.org/2017/11/how-to-excel-at-both-strategy-and-execution.

Lewis, C. S. *The Last Battle*. New York: Collier Books, 1970.

Longman, Tremper, III. *Proverbs*. Grand Rapids: Baker Academic, 2006.

Newbigin, Lesslie. *Proper Confidence: Faith, Doubt, and Certainty in Christian Discpleship*. Grand Rapids: Eerdmans, 1995.

Nonaka, Ikujiro, and Hirotaka Takeuchi. "The Big Idea: The Wise Leader." *Harvard Business Review*, May 2011. https://hbr.org/2011/05/the-big-idea-the-wise-leader.

Pascal, Blaise. *Pascal's Pensees*. New York: E. P. Dutton, 1958.

Provan, Iain. *Seriously Dangerous Religion: What the Old Testament Really Says and Why It Matters*. Waco, TX: Baylor University Press, 2014.

"Qi Rushan." *Encyclopedia Britannica*. Accessed June 7, 2023. https://www.britannica.com/biography/Qi-Rushan.

Sinek, Simon. *Start with Why: How Great Leaders Inspire Everyone to Take Action*. New York: Penguin Books, 2009.

Singh, Maanvi. "Curiosity: It Helps Us Learn, but Why?" NPR, October 24, 2014. https://www.npr.org/sections/ed/2014/10/24/357811146/curiosity-it-may-have-killed-the-cat-but-it-helps-us-learn.

Solzhenitsyn, Aleksandr. *The Gulag Archipelago, 1918–1956: An Experiment in Literary Investigation*. New York: Harper Perennial Modern Classics, 2007.

Sternberg, Robert J., and Judith Gluck, eds. *The Cambridge Handbook of Wisdom*. Cambridge: Cambridge University Press, 2019.

Sucher, Sandra J. *Herman Miller (A): Innovation by Design*. Business Case Study. Boston: Harvard Business School, 2002.

Tisby, Jemar. *The Color of Compromise*. Grand Rapids: Zondervan Reflective, 2019.

Todd, Douglas. "Meet the Creator of the 'Laughing Jesus' (Photo)." *Vancouver (BC) Sun*, January 19, 2014. https://vancouversun.com/news/staff-blogs/meet-the-creator-of-the-laughing-jesus-photo.

Tolkien, J. R. R. *Leaf by Niggle*. Dublin: HarperCollins, 2016.

———. *The Letters of J. R. R. Tolkien*. Edited by Humphrey Carpenter. New York: Houghton Mifflin, 2000.

———. *The Lord of the Rings*. New York: Houghton Mifflin, 2004.

Trueblood, Elton. *The Humor of Christ*. New York: Harper & Row, 1964.

Wright, N. T. *The New Testament and the People of God*. Minneapolis: Fortress, 1992.

INDEX

Harvard Business Review, 48, 136
Herman Miller, 51, 61, 124, 156
Holy Spirit. *See* Spirit, God's
*Humilitas: A Lost Key to Life, Love,
and Leadership* (Dickson), 45–47
humility and wisdom, 45–64; building trust and agreement when possible, 58–59; and Collins's research
on "Level 5 Leaders," 48–49;
defining, 45–47; epistemological,
36, 52, 53–54; exhibiting genuine
curiosity about others, 55–56, 72;
exhibiting vulnerability, 60–63; Jesus's examples of, 46, 47, 49, 64; in
junior people in an organization,
49–50, 62; leadership practices
that cultivate, 55–63; letting each
person define their views in a
disagreement, 57–58; owning your
own responsibility, 59–60; power
and, 46–47, 66–67, 68, 86, 101, 128;
as the primary virtue of leadership,
63–64, 101; recognizing the limits
of what we know, 36, 52–53; and
shrewdness, 48–49; two foundational attitudes for, 52–54
humor, 157–60. *See also* youthfulness (youthful curiosity and
playfulness)
Humor of Christ, The (Trueblood),
158
hyperbole, humor and, 157–60

idolatry, 12
imagination. *See* leadership
imagination
institutional power, healthy, 101–3
institutions, caring about, 99–101
introversion, 112–13
Invitation to Solitude and Silence:

*Experiencing God's Transformative
Presence* (Barton), 114
Isaac, the sacrifice of, 22, 24, 152
Isaiah (prophet), 12, 35, 75–76, 125
Israel, ancient: David's battle with
Goliath and the Philistine army,
154–55; forty years of bondage in
the wilderness, 105, 109–10; idolatry at base of Mount Sinai, 12; interdependence of God's work and the
work of, 79–80; Moses and God's
relationship with, 12–13, 167; and
Near Eastern wisdom traditions,
34; the powerless, 90; wisdom of
King Solomon, 34, 72, 160–61

Jackson, Peter, 65
James, 39–41, 64, 91, 121–22
Jeremiah (prophet), 5
Jesus: acts of power, 13, 67; Caravaggio's painting depicting the
birth of, 16; commissioning the
disciples, 162–63; concern for the
poor and weak, 12; the crucifixion,
46, 47, 115; God's embodiment in,
13, 16–18; and humility, 46, 47, 49,
64; and importance of childlikeness, 17–18, 150–51; James on the
wisdom from above, 39–41; on
participative power and metaphor
of the yoke, 80; Pilate's interro-
gation on the truth, 10; on the
possibility of eternal life, 42; response to James and John, 121–22;
resurrection encounters with the
disciples, 17–18, 86–87; on the
Sabbath, 109; sense of humor and
use of hyperbole, 157–60; Sermon
on the Mount, 38–39, 40; taking
the form of a slave, 121